Going and Growing

Going and Growing

Is Cross-Cultural Mission for You?

Dick and Thea Van Halsema

BAKER BOOK HOUSE
Grand Rapids, Michigan 49516

Contents

Preface

We were privileged to bring the nineteenth annual series of Baker Mission Lectures on the Robinson Road campus of Reformed Bible College, Grand Rapids, Michigan, in February 1990.

The roster of the seventeen speakers who preceded us as Baker mission lecturers is illustrious indeed: Arthur Glasser, Harvie M. Conn, Joel Nederhood, Edmund Clowney, Roger S. Greenway, Richard De Ridder, James I. Packer, Elisabeth Elliot, Arthur Johnston, Michael Griffiths, Robertson McQuilkin, Samuel Escobar, Jonathan Chao, Lyle Vander Werff, Ralph Winter, J. Dudley Woodberry, and Charles Van Engen. It was an honor for us to join this international group of lecturers, especially after we retired, respectively, from the RBC presidency (1966–1987) and professorship/student deanship (1972–1988).

We thank God for the late Herman Baker, founder of Baker Book House and friend of RBC, who made these mission lectures possible from their beginning in 1972. He and his son, Richard—now president of the publishing firm—underwrote costs through the years. They also published some of the presentations—those by Greenway (*Apostles to the City*) and McQuilkin (*The Great Omission*).

Together we have written these chapters as a modest encouragement for Christians, young and old, to join Christ in the worldwide mission of his church. Cross-cultural mission ministry must enlist a far greater number of workers in these closing years of the twentieth century than in the past.

We pray that God will use this book to convey what cross-cultural mission ministry requires: Christians who enter such service must have a living faith and an awareness of the church's global mission to bring the Good News of Jesus Christ to all peoples.

Such workers also must keep growing—in their relationship to Jesus Christ, in understanding themselves, and in cultivating relationships with people of a culture different from their own.

Cross-cultural mission ministry is a matter of *going and growing*.

Dick and Thea Van Halsema
Grand Rapids, Michigan

1

"Imitate Their Faith"

Dick

The New Testament letter to first-century Jewish Christians instructs its readers to imitate their spiritual leaders. "Remember your leaders, who spoke the word of God to you," we read in Hebrews 13:7. "Consider the outcome of their way of life and imitate their faith."

Think about these lines from Hebrews as you reflect about the millions of Christian witnesses and missionaries who have served Christ throughout the world in the two millennia since Pentecost. We are called to imitate their faith.

We know relatively little about this long line of evangelists and witnesses. Most of us live below the intellectual "poverty line" on the mission history awareness scale. However, we need not remain ignorant of the innumerable company of men and women through whom God has been spreading the gospel.

As we become familiar with the biographies of these pioneers, God wants us to "consider the outcome of their way of life and imitate their faith." He wants us to know about their daring, their difficulties, and their determination to make known to others the saving love of Jesus Christ the Lord—even if the price they had to pay was martyrdom.

Witnessing for Jesus Christ today, whether in a crosscultural setting or at home, requires vision—a vision of people lost without salvation through God's only Son. And it takes faith—faith that God wants to use the lives and testimonies of his people to plant saving truth in the hearts and lives of those who are to be saved.

It is difficult to select only a few missionary leaders from all the centuries past. As the writer to the Hebrews said, "We are surrounded by such a great cloud" of witnesses (12:1). But it will be good to meet some of these witnesses—seven from relatively recent years—whose lives and efforts may move us to attempt great things for God. Like hundreds of thousands of other witnesses about whom you can read, these seven made significant contributions to the spread of the gospel.

Count Nicolaus Ludwig von Zinzendorf

Count Nicolaus Ludwig von Zinzendorf, a Christian nobleman of the 1700s, lived in Saxony, an area which was part of post-World War II East Germany. Protestant Reformer Martin Luther (1483–1546) had lived and worked in this same area.

Zinzendorf had a vision of propagating the Christian faith far and wide. He opened the family estate to friends from nearby Moravia and to others who shared his mission vision.

A village came into existence called "Herrnhut"—"the Lord's shelter." Those who lived in it were called "Moravians"; their community and church became a center of missionary inspiration and outreach to many parts of the world. The Moravians' zeal for the progress of the gospel is well-known today.

Describing the Herrnhut fellowship, mission historian Kenneth Scott Latourette observed, "Here was a new phenomenon in the expansion of Christianity, an entire community . . . devoted to the propagation of the faith. Here was a fellowship of Christians . . . with the spread of the Gospel as a major objective, not of a minority of the membership, but of the group as a whole" (*History of the Expansion of Christianity,* Vol. 3, p. 47).

The Hernhutters, convinced of their corporate responsibility to spread the gospel, sent out some of their members as missionaries—first to Surinam in South America, later to other countries. The remaining members were to support the missionaries by prayer and by daily work. Even the Moravian colonists who migrated from Herrnhut to the American colonies were sent out with a dual assignment: to bring the gospel to Indians living along the Delaware River and to support Moravian missionaries elsewhere through profits earned by the sale of produce from their farms and products of their shops.

These Moravians had a vision for total commitment to missions, a vision which we need if we are to help advance the mission of Christ's church today. In some congregations, missions seem to be the concern of only a small minority of the members. An enormous expansion of mission vision and outreach would take place in our churches if we, like the Moravians, saw missions as the privilege and responsibility of the entire membership. This was the

Moravian view of missions, and their "way of life" produced measurable mission outcomes.

William Carey

William Carey was a cobbler and part-time Baptist lay preacher in London, England, 200 years ago. His life and labors greatly affected the course of the history of Christian missions as we know it today.

Brought up in a Christian family, Carey was an avid student of the Bible. He never had an opportunity to attend a Bible school or seminary. Hearing preachers refer occasionally to "the original Greek," Carey decided to learn this ancient language by himself. This he did, working through a Greek New Testament propped up on his workbench while he mended shoes.

What Carey learned from the Bible radically influenced his life. He became convinced that the Great Commission and similar passages were not limited to Christ's apostles and their immediate followers. If the biblical mission mandate remained in effect, he and fellow Christians also were obliged to spread the gospel to other people.

Carey found few church members or pastors who shared his convictions about missions. Once he spoke about his mission vision to a meeting of ministers in London. At the close of the session, the chairman told him: "Young man, if God wants to convert the heathens, He is perfectly able to do so. And He will do so without your help!"

Such opposition tended to put Carey *down* for a time, but it did not put him *off.* In 1792 he published a book of data on the population of various countries and the woefully small proportion of Christians in those lands. He gave his treatise the impressive title, "An Earnest Enquiry into the Obligation of Christians to Use Means for the Conversion of the Heathens."

Also in 1792, Carey and a few friends organized the Baptist Missionary Society. (Three years later it became the London Missionary Society, reflecting a membership broader than the Baptists.) At the first meeting of the Society, Carey preached a sermon on Isaiah 44:2–3. The sermon contained two memorable phrases which marked Carey's missionary conviction: "Expect great things from God!" "Attempt great things for God!"

Acting on his convictions, Carey and his family sailed for India in 1793. He remained there, without a single furlough, until his death forty-one years later in 1834.

Although other men and women pioneered in missionary outreach before William Carey served in India, he generally is regarded as "the Father of the Modern Mission Era." Latourette wrote that Carey was "the first Anglo-Saxon Protestant either in America or Great Britain to propose that Christians take concrete steps to bring the Gospel to all the human race" (*History of the Expansion of Christianity,* Vol. 4, pp. 67–68).

Further, Carey was a pioneer in urging members of various evangelical denominations to cooperate for the global spread of the gospel. Until his time, Anglicans, Presbyterians, Baptists, and Methodists worked independently of each other.

As a missionary, Carey was an innovator. He was the first missionary in modern times to stress that the gospel must be preached in the language of the people and that Scripture must be translated into the tongue of each language group. Amazingly, Carey personally worked on translations of all or part of the Bible into forty-four languages and dialects by 1832, all of which were printed at Serampore, India, during his lifetime.

This remarkable English cobbler-turned-missionary was the first missionary of modern times to insist that self-governing local congregations be formed among those who became Christians in each cultural group being evangelized. At the same time, he set up schools to educate mature believers who would become pastors and evangelists for their churches; their ministry and authority would replace that of the foreign missionaries as soon as possible.

Spanning nearly four decades in India, Carey's missionary labors were filled with difficulties: antagonism from British colonial authorities, problems with fellow missionaries, and the long-lasting physical and emotional illnesses of his wife. But Carey's missionary vision and "the outcome of his way of life" were remarkably used by God for the spread of the gospel. Thank God for Carey and his missionary colleagues! May we "imitate their faith" (Hebrews 13:7).

James Hudson Taylor

J. Hudson Taylor was an Englishman who founded the China Inland Mission—known today as Overseas Missionary Fellowship. In the hundred years from the middle of the nineteenth century until the Communists under Chairman Mao closed China to missionaries in the 1950s, no other organization—Roman Catholic or Protestant—sent more missionaries to China (see Latourette, *History of the Expansion of Christianity,* Vol. 6, pp. 326ff).

Taylor went to China as a missionary for the first time in 1853, when he was twenty-one years old. He stayed there until forced by ill health to return to England seven years later. But his return to England was prompted by other factors, too.

During the turbulent mid-nineteenth century years, European powers were maneuvering to force China to open its borders to Western trade and commerce. In Taylor's time, Chinese authorities officially had opened only five coastal cities and Hong Kong to foreigners. Most missionaries from Europe and North America were clustered in these ports.

Chafing under such territorial restrictions, Taylor felt a burden for preaching the gospel in the vast areas of inland China. He was unhappy with the English missionary society under whose direction he worked during his first three years in China. It was constantly in debt and expected its missionaries to make only minimal accommodation to Chinese culture.

Back in England and in poor health, Taylor completed studies for a medical degree. He also continued praying about the possibility of forming a new missionary society for China which would send workers into the interior of that huge country.

Taylor had definite characteristics in mind for the new missionary society: Its members would look to the Lord in faith for their funds, they would be drawn from all evangelical denominations, and they would be responsible for the administration of the mission on the field. Taylor referred to two Old Testament phrases which gradually became the watchwords of his new missionary society. They were "Jehovah Jireh" ("the LORD will provide," Genesis 22:14), and "Ebenezer" ("hitherto hath the LORD helped us," 1 Samuel 7:12 KJV).

. In 1865, five years after Taylor had returned to England from China, he and those who shared his faith and vision founded a new agency, the China Inland Mission. By the turn of the century, in answer to prayer and growing interest among evangelical Christians in North America as well as in Europe, the Lord drew to this mission almost one thousand men and women. These workers were dispersed as missionaries throughout the interior of China.

God was pleased to bring all this about through Taylor and his fellow workers as the fruit of their faith and "the outcome of their way of life" (Hebrews 13:7).

J. Hudson Taylor's pioneering missionary work was remarkable for many reasons. The principle of faith support was an innovation in missions, requiring each member of the China Inland Mission to look in faith to the Lord and his people for their financial support. God honored such faith, and the number of missionaries working with the new society grew steadily.

Taylor influenced mission strategy as well. Before his time, most missionary outreach was confined mainly to the coastlands of Africa, South America, and Asia. Taylor insisted that missionaries be assigned to penetrate the populous interiors of countries such as China.

Further, Taylor stressed the need for missionaries to make serious accommodation to the culture of the people whom they wanted to reach for Christ. Workers with the C.I.M. probably were required to do this more than the members of most other missionary societies at the time. They had to live among the Chinese people, not in separate mission compounds. They had to learn the language spoken by the people, wear their kind of clothing, and adopt their hairstyles. Men missionaries even had to grow a queue or "pony tail" as Chinese men did!

Another novel feature about the China Inland Mission concerned the method of conducting the affairs of the mission. Responsibility for C.I.M. administration rested in the hands of the missionaries in China—not in the hands of a mission board in a sending country, far from the actual field of work. This policy harmonized with the character of the C.I.M. as an interdenominational and international society, supported and directed by no specific denomination or particular ecclesiastical agency.

J. Hudson Taylor was a visionary whose faith bore abundant fruit for the evangelization of China's people, a fruit still being harvested today. The China Inland Mission continues today as the Overseas Missionary Fellowship, directed by James Hudson Taylor III, great-grandson of the founder. OMF missionaries are active in many areas of the Chinese dispersion outside mainland China.

Taylor's faith about reaching the unreached masses of China should inspire us to confess "Jehovah Jireh!" concerning the task of world evangelization today. Those who imitate Taylor's faith will have occasion to confess "Ebenezer" as well.

Samuel M. Zwemer

In the early 1870s a lad of Dutch extraction attended a country school house in the village of Graafschap, near Holland, Michigan. His name was Samuel Zwemer. My maternal grandfather, Dick Lucas, shared a school desk and bench with this boy who was to become a renowned missionary to the Muslim people. By the time I heard Dr. Zwemer speak in 1950 at Paterson, New Jersey (and later in Grand Rapids, Michigan), he was a missions senior statesman, the author of many books about Christian witness to Muslims, and a retired professor of missions at Princeton Seminary in New Jersey.

While an undergraduate student at Hope College in Holland, Michigan, Zwemer was impressed by a visiting speaker's chapel message about Christians' neglect of the Muslim world. Zwemer carried this concern with him to the Reformed Church Seminary at New Brunswick, New Jersey, where he studied for the ministry.

In 1888 Samuel Zwemer and two like-minded student friends offered themselves to the foreign mission board of the Reformed Church in America for service in Arabia. They were not accepted. Undeterred, Zwemer and his partners formed a new mission organization—the Arabian Mission. They began to prepare themselves for service among Muslims in the Middle East, trusting God to open the way for them to serve there.

Supported by the prayers and gifts of interested Christians, one of the three students—James Cantine—sailed in 1889 for Syria to study the Arabic language there. Samuel Zwemer caught up with him the following year. And thus a new mission to Muslim people was born.

The young mission team soon decided to make their operating base at Basrah, near the head of the Arabian Gulf. From there they traveled to bring their witness to Christ throughout the region.

Thank God, the missionary efforts of Zwemer and his friends did not go unnoticed back home in the United States. By 1894 the Reformed Church foreign mission board accepted responsibility for the Arabian Mission, and a steady growth ensued—both in the number of new missionaries and the opening of schools and hospitals. The mission still exists today.

Samuel Zwemer's missionary contribution must be seen in the context of Christian missionary expansion at the end of the nineteenth century. Large population groups such as the Buddhists, Hindus, and Muslims remained relatively untouched by missionary outreach. Each of these large religious blocs contained adherents numbering in the hundreds of millions. Yet, only a small proportion of Christian missionaries was dedicated to their evangelization.

Many Christian churches in the West seemed to be intimidated by the formidable resistance of the older religions to the gospel—whether by the pantheistic animism of the Buddhists or by the polytheistic syncretism of the Hindus. Similarly, Western Christians tended to write off attempts to evangelize Muslims because they appeared impenetrably resistant to the Good News of salvation through the Lord Jesus Christ.

Certainly, men and women who are to spend their lives as witnesses for Christ among the followers of such ancient and supposedly formidable religions must believe without a doubt that the gospel "is the power of God for the salvation of everyone who believes" (Romans 1:16).

God delights to raise up this kind of missionary. He will not be left without believing witnesses among Buddhists, Hindus, Muslims, or any other group of people. In west Michigan one hundred years ago he raised up the son of immigrant Dutch Reformed Christians, and through him the Holy Spirit initiated a new and influential witness for Christ among Muslims.

Samuel Zwemer has been called the "apostle to Islam," a "flaming prophet" who demonstrated and declared God's love to Muslims. This is what Kenneth Scott Latourette wrote: "Zwemer became one of the most famous of Christian missionaries to Muslims" in the twentieth century, "traveling over most of the Islamic world, arousing in Europe and America interest in bringing the faith to Muslims, and recruiting and training missionaries" (*History of the Expansion of Christianity,* Vol. 6, p. 61).

Like the apostle Paul, Zwemer concentrated on sowing the seed of God's Good News and leaving the results to him. Despite the paucity of visible results in Muslim evangelization, he contended that those who labor in faith and love among Muslims will share a blessed surprise when Christ returns. Undoubtedly they will see many Muslims who secretly trusted in Christ rise to life everlasting from Muslim cemeteries at the Last Day.

Johanna Veenstra

Born in 1894 to a Dutch immigrant family living near Paterson, New Jersey, Johanna Veenstra served as a pioneer missionary in Nigeria during the 1920s and early 1930s. Johanna was an inspiration both to the people in Nigeria among whom she worked and to her supporters in the churches at home.

Johanna's father was a carpenter who became a preacher. In 1902, during the first year of his first pastorate at the rural Christian Reformed Church of Zutphen, Michigan, he died. Johanna was a child at the time. Her widowed mother moved back to Paterson with her six small children and raised them there.

During World War I Johanna commuted daily from Paterson to her job as a secretary in New York City. Apparently, she was restless about her religious upbringing and cultural background. She thought about disassociating herself from the faith of her family and about seeking her future away from childhood surroundings.

Providentially, the Lord meant otherwise for Johanna. He brought her to a saving faith in himself and planted in her heart the call to missionary service. While studying at a mission training school in New York City, she developed a keen interest in the vast number of the world's people who had heard little or nothing about Christ or God's Word. She applied for missionary appointment to Africa with the Sudan United Mission based in England. But she was considered too young to be assigned to foreign mission service.

Looking for an opportunity to serve in her own country, Johanna Veenstra returned to Michigan. In Grand Rapids, she worked in a city mission while attending classes at Calvin Preparatory School (which later became Calvin College).

The end of World War I in 1918 led Johanna once again to consider going to Nigeria. Friends counseled her that this plan might be unrealistic. After all, her denomination—the Christian Reformed Church—at that time was not sending missionaries abroad, to Nigeria or any other country.

Johanna probably learned that the Christian Reformed synod in 1918 appointed a committee to recommend a country to which the denomination should send its first missionaries overseas. Reporting to the next synod in 1920, the committee recommended that the church's first foreign missionaries should be sent to Nigeria. Unexpectedly, however, the synod rejected the committee's recommendation. The assembly voted instead to send the denomination's first foreign missionaries to China.

Johanna Veenstra was disappointed by this turn of events, but she remained convinced that her desire to be a missionary in Nigeria was inspired by God. For a second time, she applied to the Sudan United Mission for appointment. This time Johanna was accepted.

During the 1920s and early 1930s, Johanna Veenstra brought the gospel to many people living in Nigeria's interior. Joining her British missionary colleagues, she learned a new language, adapted to a new culture, endured privations, and battled disease. She traveled by bicycle or trekked on foot to set up Bible classes, provide primary medical care, establish churches, and organize schools.

While she was serving Christ in the interior of Nigeria, "Johanna of Nigeria" became a household name to hundreds of Christian Reformed families across America. Sunday school children were told about her pioneering work for Christ in the heart of Africa. Personally, I remember Miss Veenstra's visit to our family home in the early 1930s, while I was growing up in a Passaic, New Jersey parsonage not far from the Veenstra home in Paterson.

In 1933 sad news came from Nigeria. Only a few days before her thirty-ninth birthday Johanna Veenstra died unexpectedly after surgery in a mission hospital at Mayango. She was buried in a lonely cemetery near the village of Vom. In 1985, fifty-two years after Johanna went to heaven, we visited the house in Lupwe, Plateau State, where she had made her home. We found that she and her labor have not been forgotten.

Johanna's impact for missions did not end with her relatively early death. Not too many years later, her own denomination—the Christian Reformed Church—decided to send missionaries to Nigeria. Many men and women came to follow in Johanna's pioneering footsteps. After World War II, Nigeria became the denomination's largest mission field. Today the so-called "daughter churches" in Johanna Veenstra's adopted country number more members than do the "mother churches" in North America!

God greatly honored the faith of Johanna Veenstra and her unconditional dedication to bring the gospel to the people of

Nigeria. Such faith and dedication were God's gift to her, and he has not stopped giving such gifts to his people today.

Two-thirds of the world's people—approximately 3.5 billion of them—remain outside of Christ, and their numbers continue to increase. Who will imitate Johanna's faith? The outcome of her way of life was that many Nigerians came to know the Savior of the world. With respect to the progress of the gospel, what will be the outcome of our lives?

Leonard Livingston Legters and William Cameron Townsend

Two hundred years ago William Carey urged fellow Christians to think globally about missions. One hundred years ago J. Hudson Taylor called missionaries to move beyond the coastlines of the great continents to evangelize the vast populations inland.

Not until the twentieth century was the goal of reaching countries and continents surpassed by a new, more specific goal—namely, the need to evangelize particular "people groups." This term came increasingly into use after Ralph Winter, then a faculty member at Fuller Seminary's School of World Mission in Pasadena, California, spoke on this theme at the 1974 Congress on World Evangelization held at Lausanne, Switzerland.

After Winter's speech at Lausanne, churches and mission agencies began to adopt the "people group" concept, for strategy purposes as well as terminology. Even the members of many churches caught up the phrase. Consequently, they realized that it no longer was explicit enough to talk about "our missionaries in Mexico," for example. After all, Mexico is a large nation with possibly 175 distinct languages and dialects. Each represents a unique culture and people—many of whom are unevangelized.

Earlier in this century God led two missionaries (among others) to focus their work on specific "people groups," long before that phrase was coined. One was Leonard Livingston Legters, a Dutch-background resident of New York state who became a Hope College alumnus. The other was William Cameron Townsend, of Scottish ancestry, who studied at Occidental College in California.

L. L. Legters first served as a Reformed Church missionary pastor among Comanche Indians in Oklahoma, next as a Presbyterian minister on the U. S. East Coast, and then as an itinerant speaker at church mission conferences. He made survey trips along the Amazon River in Brazil and elsewhere to document the spiritual needs of numerous language groups. Then he would challenge churches back home to pray and to act for the evangelization of these unreached people.

In the 1920s Rev. Legters made an extensive missionary survey trip on horseback through Central America, riding through Guatemala to Mexico. A year later, he spoke at a Bible conference in Guatemala to a Cakchiquel Indian audience. His messages underwent double translation—first into Spanish by missionary W. Cameron Townsend, and then into Cakchiquel by an Indian translator.

Townsend had come from California to Guatemala in 1917 to sell Bibles, assuming that Spanish was the national language. How surprised he had been to discover that most of the indigenous people spoke only their mother tongue! Few of these people could read or understand the Spanish Scriptures which Townsend was trying to sell to them.

An often-described incident startled Townsend and spurred him to think about the translation needs of unreached people groups. He was trying to sell a Spanish New Testament to a

Cakchiquel Indian. The man retorted, "If your God, the God of this book, is so great, why can't He speak our language?" Townsend began to wonder how a Cakchiquel translation of the New Testament could be produced.

Townsend shared his burden about Bibleless people in Guatemala with L. L. Legters—the Bible conference speaker in 1921. The two men got along well. Townsend told Legters about his growing awareness that Bible translations were needed for each of Guatemala's distinct language groups, such as the Cakchiquels among whom he was working.

Legters, in turn, amazed Townsend by reporting about the hundreds of unevangelized language groups which he had seen and heard about in South and Central America alone—none of whom had a single page of God's Word. He also mentioned the countless unreached groups reportedly living in other parts of the world.

The two men talked and prayed about the obvious need for thousands of new Bible translations. By faith, they determined to do something about this pressing need.

Townsend, keenly aware that he lacked academic preparation for work in the field of linguistics, agreed to work on a Cakchiquel translation of the New Testament. Legters agreed to promote the cause of unreached peoples and to raise money for Townsend's Cakchiquel translation project as he itinerated to speak at church mission conferences in the United States. Keeping his part of the bargain, Legters set up a new organization called the "Pioneer Mission Agency."

Out of these small beginnings by Legters and Townsend, the Summer Institute of Linguistics was born in 1935. It also was known subsequently among Christians in supporting countries as Wycliffe Bible Translators. Today, SIL members are at work in many countries—preparing Scripture portions, New Testaments, and occasionally complete Bibles in hundreds of languages. With about six thousand members drawn from many countries, Wycliffe is the largest non-denominational evangelical mission agency in the world today.

L. L. Legters died a half century ago. His son, Dr. David Brainerd Legters Sr., worked on the translation of the New Testament into the language of eastern Mexico's Maya people.

Until he died in 1983, W. Cameron Townsend remained active in the cause of providing God's Word for "every man in his own tongue." His trips took him to many parts of the earth—including the Soviet Union. Through his vision, his love for people (which opened the way for him to meet the leaders of many nations as well as the members of many indigenous, preliterate groups), and his persistence in recruiting translators for Bibleless tribes, "Uncle Cam" publicized the needs of unreached people groups far and wide.

What makes the example of Legters and Townsend so significant for us today? The answer lies not in their pioneering spirit, their personal gifts, their academic accomplishments, or their knack of getting along with all kinds of people.

The secret of their accomplishments was their faith—faith in God and in his word, a faith by which they could envision what God wants his people to do and what he will help them to accomplish as they trust him.

Townsend's conviction about the indispensability of a living faith in God and in his Word is heard clearly in a stanza from his favorite hymn:

> Faith, mighty faith the promise sees
> And looks to God alone,
> Laughs at impossibilities
> And shouts, "It shall be done!"[1]

Conclusion

By faith Nicolaus von Zinzendorf taught that mission is the task of the entire congregation. By faith, William Carey called the Christians of his day to see the global dimensions of their missionary obligation. By faith, J. Hudson Taylor saw that the gospel message must penetrate entire nations.

By faith Samuel Zwemer believed God that Muslims can be brought to know the saving love of God in Jesus Christ by the power of the Holy Spirit. By faith Johanna Veenstra followed the vision of missionary service all the way to Nigeria, even when her own denomination was not prepared to send her. By faith Legters and Townsend took steps which launched a global movement to provide the Word of God for every tribe in its own tongue.

God calls us to follow the example of these witnesses. He wants us to "consider the outcome of their way of life and imitate their faith" (Hebrews 13:7). For the mission of Christ's church today, what will be the outcome of our way of life, the fruit of our faith?

> By faith we walk, and not by sight,
> By faith we know and do the right;
> > By faith we learn,
> > By faith we love,
> By faith we please our God above.
>
> By faith we trust what He ordains,
> By faith we find His grace sustains;
> > By faith we serve,
> > By faith we go,
> By faith we live our life below.[2]

2

"Attempt Great Things for God"

Dick

J esus was not mincing his words. He was sitting with his disciples on the Mount of Olives, the panorama of Jerusalem and the temple mount spread out to the west in front of them. In response to questions from his disciples about the future, Jesus was talking about the end of the world and his coming again (Matthew 24:3–14).

Jesus predicted the coming of three cosmic catastrophes—wars, famines, and earthquakes—but he said that these would not be the worst of impending calamities. More troublesome would be the "ten woes" affecting the church itself—*six woes* from outside the church, *four woes* from within the church. Jesus described the six external woes as persecution, death, hatred, falsehood, deception, and increasing wickedness in the world. The four internal woes predicted by Jesus are apostasy, betrayal or treason within the fellowship, hatred of one another, and coldness.

We might say that Jesus is sketching a tremendously gloomy scenario. But he is not finished with his prophetic statements. The three cosmic catastrophes and the ten woes, Jesus says, are followed by the three promises of verses 13 and 14:

> But he who stands firm to the end will be saved.
> And this gospel of the kingdom will be preached in the whole world as a testimony to
>   all nations,
> And then the end will come.

Concerned as we are with the spread of the gospel throughout the world, we must reckon realistically with our Lord's disclosures about the hostility of the world and the weaknesses of the church. Both are evident today.

But we must rivet our attention especially on the exciting promises which Christ gives about those who persevere in the faith, about the progress of the gospel, and about the certainty of his "parousia" (his return, appearing) at the end of the age. These three promises are the divine certainties that make missions possible.

All this is mirrored in the progress of world evangelization and the planting of the church. More people than ever inhabit planet earth, but more people on all continents also worship God through his Son than ever before.

By the year A.D. 2000 the majority of Africa's people may be Christian. By the close of the twentieth century, evangelicals may outnumber Roman Catholics in Latin America. A dynamic spiritual awakening appears to be under way in sections of Asia—in South Korea, in the house churches of rural China, and in parts of Indonesia. And in the Soviet Union, an increasing Christian community—said to exceed the numbers of Christians in North America—is thanking

God for unprecedented freedoms, as *glasnost* and *pere-stroika* replace Communist enmity with respect to religion.

A survey of world missions today reveals numerous significant trends which must be seen in the light of Jesus' revelations about the future of the church. Three global factors related to world evangelization deserve our attention: (1) the growth of world population, (2) the response of the Christian church to the mission mandate, and (3) the state of the Christian mission today.

The Growth of World Population

The growth of world population continues unabated. The link between this growth and world missions should be plain for all to see; it rules out any talk about merely maintaining the missions status quo—let alone adopting a missions moratorium.

Consider the accelerating rate of global population growth during the past twenty centuries. When Jesus was on earth, perhaps 250 million people were alive. Seventeen hundred years passed before the total number of human beings increased to one billion. That many people apparently were on earth around 1775, when the American colonies were engaged in a revolution against England.

The two-billion mark was registered around 1870, approximately one hundred years later. Then, only seventy years passed before the human family numbered three billion people in 1940, on the eve of World War II. Twenty-six years later, despite the death and devastation which that war brought about, the total reached four billion.

In November 1966, I attended the first Congress on World Evangelization in West Berlin. A prominent feature in the main lobby of the Kongresshalle near the Brandenburg Gate was a large electronic device called "the people counter." During the ten-day congress the digital display registered the steadily-increasing number of people on earth.

Called to the lobby one evening, congress participants watched as the digits on the huge odometer-like display changed from 3,999,999,999 to 4 billion. Congress chairman Billy Graham briefly reminded us that the task of world evangelization, humanly speaking, was expanding by the hour.

Only twenty-one years later, the United Nations announced that the earth was home to more than five billion people. And today another four hundred million persons have swelled the total. In fact, half of the people who ever have lived on earth are living today!

More than one billion people live in the People's Republic of China. Another billion are found in the Indian subcontinent—in Pakistan, India, and Bangladesh. Africa and South America together account for almost a third billion inhabitants. An estimated world population of 6.2 billion is expected by the year 2000.

With 5.2 billion people now living on our planet, the implications for the mission of Christ's church are obvious and inescapable. Consider what would happen if every one of the world's 1.7 Christians would lead at least one other person to Christ. Then a total of 3.4 billion persons would be followers of Jesus the Messiah. But 1.8 billion other people would remain unreached, simply because they have no Christian neighbors.

Statistically, all of the 1.8 billion unreached people could be contacted personally with the gospel if at least 360,000 Christians would leave their homes to become cross-cultural missionaries to live among them for Christ's sake. But the goal would be reached only if each of the 360,000 new missionaries could present Christ to at least 5,000 persons who do not know him. Happily, this probably is not God's strategy for reaching everyone on earth. But this hypothetical plan does emphasize the enormity of the task. It also highlights our responsibility as the Lord's people to act as well as to pray for world evangelization.

Other aspects of current population trends are worth noting. During the last decade, the number of people living south of the equator has exceeded those living north of it for the first time in history. At the same time, whites have become a decided minority among earth's peoples. Also, the average age of the population in many parts of the "Two-Thirds World" is only fifteen—a condition with a potential for even more rapid population growth.

Of course, future population levels will be subject to many variables: war, famine, plague, and natural catastrophes. The Sovereign God who will see that the mission of Christ's church is completed will direct the affairs of men and nations to conform to his plans for today and tomorrow.

David Barrett is a leader among the new breed of mission researchers who are accumulating an amazing amount of missionary statistics. They point out that a prominent feature of the world's burgeoning population is the migration to large cities on all continents.

In 1900 the world had 400 cities with more than 100,000 inhabitants each. Today, the number of such cities is over 3,370. Again, in 1900, demographers could account for only twenty *megacities* (a term describing centers of over one million people). Today, the list includes 320 such megacities.

The sheer size of today's great cities often defies comprehension. The Mexico City metropolitan area, with the largest urban population in the world, has more people than the continent of Australia. Also, its population is larger than that of Canada, Malaysia, Nepal, or the Netherlands!

The world's urban centers—small, medium, large, and extra large—constitute the greatest challenge to Christian missions of all time. Except in Korea and Japan, megacities generally are multi-ethnic, a majority of the residents are poor, and many of the families are broken. In such "world class" concentrations of people, numerous new forms of the church are emerging.

In its issue of January 22, 1990, *Time* magazine published an interview with Peter Drucker, the American business and management authority. In it, Drucker predicted the coming decline of urban growth around the world. He said, "I think that we have seen the last outburst of the city as we know it." His argument is that huge cities have become so untraversable, unmanageable, and unliveable that the human tide is bound to flow away from them rather than to them.

Whether or not Drucker's guess comes true, almost half of the world's people now live in cities. The men, women, and children who crowd into them need the Lord. Most of them are without the True Shepherd, and the Lord Jesus wants us to have compassion on them. This was the thrust of Baker Mission Lectures given by Dr. Roger S. Greenway in 1976 at Reformed Bible College, Grand Rapids, Michigan. These lectures were published by Baker Book House under the title *Apostles to the City.*

Jesus promised his disciples that the "gospel of the kingdom shall be preached in the whole world." This includes the cities. Many more willing witnesses and workers are needed if the cities are to be reached for Christ.

The Response of the Christian Church

A concern for the progress of the gospel whets our appetites for information about the missionary response and spiritual health of the Christian church. It is good to read that the number of Christians in the world is larger than ever before. However, the same must be said about the number of non-Christians.

According to researcher David Barrett, the number of Christians in the world at the beginning of 1991 was almost 1.8 billion—out of 5.4 billion people. The three largest Christian communities are the Roman Catholic, Protestant, and Orthodox—in that order. One third of the world's people are Christian, but the percentage in urban areas is higher—over 48 percent. The latter fact should brighten the prospects for fruitful evangelistic activities in cities.

Thank God, evangelical churches and their members in many places are increasingly dedicated to the task of evangelizing their neighbors. They also are taking a more substantial role in world missions, both in terms of financial support and in encouraging likely candidates to prepare for missionary vocations.

At the same time, the greater part of the international Christian community remains largely uninvolved in the mission of Christ's church. The lack of dedication among these congregations and their members raises questions about the spiritual health of the church. It also is reflected in the financial stewardship exercised by Christians. Do you realize that in 1988 Christians around the world had an estimated aggregate income of 8.5 trillion U.S. dollars? To put it differently, that amounted to 8.5 million millions of dollars.

Yet, Christians gave less than 1.8 percent of these trillions of dollars to Christian ministries. Only one tenth of 1 percent (or 8.3 billion dollars) was contributed to world missions. These figures reveal that missionary outreach is far from being a top priority for many Christians. We spend one thousand times as much money for material goods as we do for the progress of the gospel.

The global Christian church encompasses wide diversity within itself. Large parts of the church are bound by tradition which is centuries old and have undergone little or no change despite radical change taking place in the world around them. Meanwhile, other parts of the church—both Roman and Protestant—have experienced new life through Pentecostal or charismatic influences.

Johannes Verkuyl was a Dutch Reformed missionary who was sent from churches in the Netherlands to Indonesia. He later succeeded Johan Bavinck as professor of missions at the Free University of Amsterdam in the mid-1960s. Writing in the *International Bulletin of Missionary Research* for April 1989, Verkuyl observed that most churches of the West one century ago displayed a measure of fervor for missionary outreach which was marked by a spirit of triumphalism. The churches were confident about their missionary competence. This attitude continued as long as they could subject the *younger churches* to the paternalistic control of the *older churches*.

After World War II, Verkuyl observes, rapid change took place in the mission outlook of the Western churches. They were forced to relinquish their controls over mission churches as the spirit of nationalism rose and the era of colonialism ended. This shift of power between the so-called *older* and *younger* churches opened the way for a shared missionary responsibility—which Verkuyl calls *polycentric* rather than *monocentric*. Because of this shift, mission responsibility now is exercised from many geographical centers, such as Jakarta, Lagos, Tokyo, and Buenos Aires—not merely from Amsterdam or Geneva or New York.

Now some churches of the West, Verkuyl continues, having shifted from missions *triumphalism* to *polycentrism,* have begun to demonstrate an almost total retreat or paralysis with respect to mission activity.

To illustrate: Forty years ago, the three major Presbyterian denominations in the United States supported 2,000 missionaries. Today, they sponsor fewer than 500 missionaries, 88 percent of whom are near retirement age. Other denominations have concluded that the day of international missionary outreach is past and that the time for a "missions moratorium" has come.

Western Europe, the stronghold of the Christian faith a few centuries ago but described as post-Christian since World War II, once again is being recognized as a mission field. This was the consensus of Christian mission leaders from twenty-one countries who met at Stuttgart, West Germany, in September 1988.

Arthur F. Glasser, Dean Emeritus of the School of World Mission at Fuller Theological Seminary in Pasadena, California, writes about "the Stuttgart Call," which conferees endorsed as their meeting concluded. The document says to the church around the world:

> Come over and help us! We Christians in Europe confess that we need to learn from the churches in Africa, Asia, and the Americas in their unself-conscious, winsome ways of sharing the abundant life of Christ. So we invite the church worldwide to work with us in partnership for the re-evangelization of our continent and the evangelization of the areas and peoples in our countries which are still unreached. (*International Bulletin of Missionary Research,* January 1989)

The United States often has been called a Christian country. It sobers us to learn, however, that it actually is one of the world's largest mission fields. Over one half of its residents are strangers to Christ. It is striking to note that possibly more Christian believers live in the Soviet Union than in the United States of America!

The State of the Christian Mission Today

Reformed Christians confess the following about the essence of Christian missions:

> The Son of God, out of the whole human race, from the beginning to the end of the world, gathers, defends, and preserves for Himself, by His Spirit and Word, in the unity of the true faith, a church chosen to everlasting life. (*Heidelberg Catechism,* Lord's Day XXI)

The relentless redeeming activity of God's Son, described in this passage of the Heidelberg Catechism, is dramatically evident today. Workers are being sent out by God in answer to the prayers of his people. The gospel is making unprecedented progress in many countries, people are being born again, and churches are being planted. Sometimes all this is accomplished through the work of expatriate missionaries and mission agencies—but sometimes in spite of them.

Arthur Glasser had this to say about the future role of mission agencies that exist today:

> Of course, we believe that the work of Jesus Christ in the midst of God's people will continue. But evangelicals have no grounds for assuming that the mission agencies of today will automatically be the strategic vehicles God will be using as the church enters its third millennium. (*International Bulletin of Missionary Research,* January 1989)

A Sober Appraisal

Glasser makes the foregoing observation about mission agencies which fail to promote the progress of the gospel. They may fail because they lack the spiritual vitality, evangelistic concern, cultural sensitivity, and administrative flexibility which effective mission ministry requires.

Jonathan Bonk, who was born in Ethiopia of missionary parents and served there several years as an adult missionary, teaches now at a Mennonite seminary in Winnipeg, Manitoba. He warns us that many Western missionaries today are not free from the influence of materialism. In the October 1989 issue of the *International Bulletin of Missionary Research,* Bonk wrote, "Western missionaries today constitute part of a rich elite whose numbers, relative to the burgeoning populations of poor around the world, constitute a steadily diminishing proportion of the world's total population."

Writing under the title, "Missions and Mammon: Six Theses," Bonk described the relative affluence of many Western missionaries and their addiction to material comforts on the field. Their subjection to such comforts is seen, for example, when North American missionaries insist that their living quarters in a "Two-Thirds World" country should be similar to middle-class houses in Toronto or Grand Rapids. By requiring such comforts abroad, they identify with the living standards of diplomats and executives of multinational corporations, the only people who can afford to have washers, clothes dryers, multi-bedroom houses with air conditioning, and two-car garages in their overseas locations.

Professor Bonk contends that every aspect of Christian missions should be influenced by three New Testament motifs: the incarnation, the cross, and the secret of power

through weakness. Our missionary witness must be shaped
and empowered by our conformity to Christ. He was *the missionary* who emptied himself of heavenly position and possessions through his incarnation. At the same time, he laid aside
his heavenly power through his sacrifice on the cross and his
burial in the grave. Who among us should be unwilling to
empty himself or herself to make Christ known to others?

As recently as the 1980s, an estimated 90 percent of
Western missionaries were concentrated in areas of the
world where the Christian church already has been planted.
However, this "hiving" of missionaries has begun to decline
as mission agencies change their strategies and disperse
mission personnel among unreached people groups.

Even then, missionaries from the West tend to have
problems in key areas. They find it difficult to identify cul-
turally with the people whom they have come to evangelize. They are slow to cooperate with evangelical churches
and missions other than their own. Further, they are reluctant to lay aside the paternalism and feelings of cultural
superiority which missionaries are apt to bring with them
from North America or Europe.

Many mission agencies in the West now seek partnership
with national churches abroad as the desired way to promote the spread of the Gospel. Some agencies, however,
still view the administration of missionary efforts abroad as
a one-way street—with churches and national missions in
countries of the "Two-Thirds World" on the receiving end.
Such relationships must be replaced with genuine two-way
cooperation in all aspects of the missionary enterprise.

To the degree that outmoded relationships between
"First World" mission agencies and "Two-Thirds World"
churches do exist, the progress of the gospel will be inhib-
ited, unreached peoples will not be sought with urgency,
and the global mission of Christ's church will be crippled.

Johannes Verkuyl has said:

> The gospel of the kingdom should be preached from decade
> to decade. In every nation there are thousands and even
> millions who have not been reached with the gospel. . . .
> This is not the time [for] the "gospel of the moratorium."
> . . . This is the time for a new initiative *in cooperation* to
> reach those who have not yet heard the gospel. (*International Bulletin of Missionary Research,* April 1989)

Difficult as it may be, Western missionaries must give up
the exercise of power and authority over national churches
where these churches exist. Mission societies must work
with and through them.

Many Exciting Developments

Despite the problems which continue to dog the church in
executing its global mission, many exciting developments are
under way today. It is true that we probably live at a time of
the greatest mission activity in two thousand years.

Great optimism about missions prevailed from the days of
William Carey at the close of the eighteenth century to the
time of World War II in the middle of the twentieth. Then the
mood changed. Chairman Mao slammed shut the door of
China to foreign missionaries in 1950 and imprisoned Chinese
pastors. Many former colonies of Western powers became
independent countries, rejecting some customs of their former masters along with their rule.

At the same time, many members of so-called "mainline"
denominations in North America and in Europe fell prey to growing uncertainty about God, the Bible, and the uniqueness of Jesus
Christ as the only Savior. This also was the age when the English
bishop Robinson published his provocative book, *God Is Dead.*

Today, however, a new optimism pervades the Christian mission around the world. This revival stems in part from one of the most important trends—the "internationalization" of world missions. Arthur Glasser calls this trend in the missionary movement "the great new fact of our time."

On this theme, Rene Padilla writes from Buenos Aires, Argentina:

> I can hardly think of the Christian mission in the 1990s without thinking of one of the most amazing changes that has been taking place since the beginning of this century, namely, the shift of the center of gravity of Christianity from the West to the two-thirds world. Of all the factors that will shape the life and mission of the church during the last decade of the twentieth century, this will undoubtedly be the predominant one.

At this point, Padilla quotes German writer Walbert Bühlmann on this theme of change in the Christian world mission:

> The Third Church has arrived. This is *the* major event of church history in the near future. To sum up in a few words: the first millennium of Christianity was the age of the First Church, the church of the East. In the second millennium the stage was held by the Second Church, the church of the West. The forms Christianity takes in the coming third millennium will in the main be determined by the Third Church, the church of the southern hemisphere—Latin America, Africa, Asia. (*International Bulletin of Missionary Research,* October 1989)

"The great new fact of our time"—the internationalization of world missions—is seen dramatically in statistics about evangelical missionary personnel now serving on the field. In the past, these workers have been drawn mainly from "the First World," Europe and North America. Today approximately 75,000 evangelical missionaries from these continents are in service around the earth.

Lawrence Keyes has made a study of the countries from which missionaries are sent. In his book *The Third Wave,* Keyes recalls that in 1972 about 3,600 non-Western missionaries were in service. In 1980 the total had nearly tripled—to 10,000 non-Western workers. Larry Keyes' associate, Jerry Pate, reports that this number continues to increase. In his book *From Every Nation,* Pate states that by 1989 the number of non-Western missionaries had risen to 36,000 men and women—about one-half of the number of "First World" missionaries.

Some mission leaders now predict that by the mid-1990s the global mission enterprise may involve more non-Western evangelical missionaries than those from the West. To repeat: "Two-Thirds World" missionaries will outnumber those from the "First World."

The impact on missions of this radical and welcome change is not hard to imagine. Undoubtedly, the Christian message will be perceived in a better light by many of its hearers because the band of witnesses will be far more international in terms of personnel and sponsorship. Further, many new mission societies will emerge, while numerous new models of mission ministry are bound to appear.

The Goal of A.D. 2000

The new optimism concerning the progress of the gospel is apparent also in the fascination of many mission leaders with the year 2000, the end of the second millennium of the Christian era. In 1987 the guest speaker for the annual Baker Mission Lectures at Reformed Bible College was Ralph Winter, Director of the U.S. Center for World Mission in Pasadena, California. He delivered five lectures on the theme, "Missions and the End of History." Dr. Winter proposed that churches and mission agencies across the world make an unparalleled effort to achieve "missionary closure" by A.D. 2000. That is, he advocated an unprecedented cooperation on the part of Christians in all countries and on all continents in an effort to complete world evangelization by the year 2000.

Winter pointed out that one hundred years ago, a similar appeal was made to U.S. Christians as the end of the nineteenth century approached. Arthur T. Pierson, Presbyterian minister, was a key leader at that time. He appealed to Christians for greater involvement in world evangelization just as Winter and others are doing as the end of another millennium approaches.

Plans for the evangelization of the world by A.D. 2000 have proliferated. In 1988 David Barrett and James Reapsome published *Seven Hundred Plans to Evangelize the World.* The book covers the nineteen centuries from Pentecost to the present day. Barrett and Reapsome point out that two-thirds of the 700 plans which were spawned have expired. However, about 250 of these plans still are afloat today.

Many of the plans for completing world evangelization by the year 2000 have been criticized unmercifully, and with good reason. Arthur Glasser observed, "One begins to wonder whether American corporate triumphalism is not taking over the evangelical empire!" (*International Bulletin of Missionary Research,* January 1989). Others scoff at "the very idea of Christian[s] . . . running megaplans in the name of world evangelization" (Raymond Fung, *International Bulletin of Missionary Research,* October 1989).

However, some eminently worthwhile "fall-out" is being recorded as a result of these A.D. 2000 mission plans. For example, the world's major evangelical broadcasters have started joint research and global planning for the first time. World Radio Missionary Fellowship (HCJB), Trans World Radio, and Far East Broadcasting Company hope to saturate the earth with gospel broadcasts in all major trade languages of the world by the year 2000.

Another "spin-off" of the suggestion that A.D. 2000 be the target date for "missionary closure" is reported by Dr. Glasser from the Far East. More than 4,000 Indonesian evangelical leaders attended a mission conference in 1988. After several days of earnest prayer and prolonged discussion, they

> pledged themselves to share the gospel with every person in their country by the year 2000 and also to train at least 5,000 to serve in other countries as evangelists and church planters. (*International Bulletin of Missionary Research,* January 1989)

Glasser's comment is apropos: "One should neither downplay nor underestimate the desire of Christians to obey their Lord's last command."

None of us want to be numbered among the skeptics and critics when Christ's disciples today increasingly pray and plan for greater obedience to the mission mandate of their Lord. An evening prayer meeting on this subject was held in a West Berlin hotel room during the 1966 Congress on World Evangelization. Several South Korean pastors invited a number of us who were housed in adjacent rooms to join them in prayer for a very specific goal. They described how they and many of South Korea's churches were praying for the Lord to *double* the number of Christian believers in their country in the next ten years.

Less than ten years later, I was amazed to hear a report that the prayer of South Korean believers was being answered. In fact, the goal was being surpassed! Today, over one-fourth of the 45 million South Korean people profess to know Christ and the growth of the church continues.

We live in a time of the greatest missionary activity in two thousand years. Who knows how great the harvest of the current decade will be—if we "expect great things from God" and also "attempt great things for God" (as did William Carey two centuries ago)?

Johannes Verkuyl's words provide a fitting finale for this chapter:

> If we should miss or dismiss the promise and the presence of the crucified and risen Lord in the continuation of missionary work, our task would be a lost cause, a meaningless enterprise. We would make concessions to the professional pessimists who think it is their task to spread alarm and defeatism.

> But within the light of the Lord's command and promise, the continuation of the church's mission in the last decade of this century will not be a lost cause or a meaningless enterprise, since we know that in the Lord our labor cannot be in vain. (*International Bulletin of Missionary Research,* April 1989)

3

Move Out of Your Fears

Dick

In the spring of 1983, Robertson McQuilkin, president of Columbia (South Carolina) Bible College and Graduate School of Bible and Missions visited Reformed Bible College in Grand Rapids, Michigan to present the twelfth annual series of Baker Mission Lectures.

From a lifelong involvement in missions—including twelve years of missionary service in Japan—President McQuilkin asked why Christ's Great Commission captures the enthusiasm and enlists the service of so few Christians.

The speaker stated his own conclusions about why mission laborers are in such short supply. McQuilkin ventured to say that, in general, Christians have "heart trouble" (Christians do not love, do not really care about those who are outside of Christ). We have "eye trouble" (we do not see the plentiful harvest on the one hand and the shortage of workers on the other).

McQuilkin continued: "We have head trouble" (that is, something is wrong with our thinking processes, our brains, when we spend most of our time in theological speculation instead of engaging in witness and evangelization). Again, the guest speaker charged that Christians are prone to have "knee trouble" (for many, prayer is a neglected means of grace) and "ear trouble" (God calls, but we do not listen or obey).

President McQuilkin's main point was that many Christians have exchanged the "Great Commission" for the "great omission" (see the lectures published by Baker Book House, Grand Rapids: *The Great Omission,* 1984).

Why do men and women who know Christ, who confess him as Savior and Lord, who love him and say that they are willing to follow wherever he leads, who know that at least 3.5 billion people need to hear about the only mediator between God and men—why do they shrink back from enlisting for missionary service?

The reticence of Christians for missionary service has puzzled me for over forty years. A military recruiter would classify as unfit for duty any person who was plagued with bad heart, eyes, head, ears, or knees. In a similar way, we could not expect people to be fit for missionary service if they are spiritually weak, blind, incompetent, deaf, or lame!

However, most Christians are not *spiritually* decrepit and unfit for duty for their Lord. The Holy Spirit indwells them and they have received spiritual gifts which they are to use in the service of Christ's body, the church.

What, then, holds Christians back from missionary involvement? This question often perplexes me at the close of the annual Mexico Summer Training Session, "STS"—an academic and practical orientation to Christian missions in a cross-cultural setting which I direct. Participants meet in Mexico City at the close of the two-month training course for a time of review and commitment.

For more than eight weeks, these men and women have shared daily Bible study and prayer, mission lectures and readings, home stays with Mexican Christian families, and field work assignments. They return at the close of this program praising God for all they have been permitted to see, learn, and do.

Yet, during the concluding commitment service in Mexico, most participants hesitate to say, "Here am I, Lord, send me!" Despite their awareness of the obvious need for great numbers of additional missionaries around the world, they appear reluctant to commit themselves to mission service for either short- or long-term duration.

Obviously, some Christians are not meant by the Lord to serve as cross-cultural missionaries. Others may be led to a commitment for such service at a later date. The climax of a summer missionary training program in Mexico may not be God's time for them to enlist for missionary service.

Nevertheless, other reasons underlie the reluctance of knowledgeable Christians to enter mission vocations. Church growth studies conducted in many countries reveal a surprising phenomenon: About one-tenth of all Christians (as well as one-tenth of a local congregation's membership) have gifts for evangelistic and missionary service. This proportion holds fairly constant whether the information is obtained in Japan, Nigeria, Mexico, the U.S., or Canada.

Since most participants in the Mexico summer mission training program are adults of college age and above, who presumably come from the one-tenth of all Christians with evangelistic gifts, should not a majority of these trainees be ready to sign up for missionary vocations? Why are they reluctant to do so?

Identifying the Fear Factor

A key reason for adult mission trainees' reluctance may be fear—fear of the unknown, and fear of the known. Sometimes a person is said to be "paralyzed with fear." In this sense, many Christians seem to be immobilized at the prospect of missionary service, regarding it as a form of hazardous duty to which they are reluctant to commit themselves. How wonderful it would be if they, with David, could testify: "The LORD is my light and my salvation—whom shall I fear? The LORD is the stronghold of my life—of whom shall I be afraid?" (Psalm 27:1).

Possibly, the "fear factor" keeps many Christians from making unconditional commitment to missionary service. The comments they make can be summarized as follows:

1. *I don't know if I could survive on the mission field.* If I were to become a missionary, I would have to leave my family, my friends, my job, my standard of living. I'm afraid of what would happen if I went so far away for so long and left everything behind.

2. *I don't know if I could adjust to a new culture and learn a second language.* I have a hard enough time learning to speak my own language correctly! I'm afraid that I would have a bad case of culture shock.

3. *I don't know where the money would come from.* Most missionary assignments require applicants to

raise their own financial support. My home church isn't used to that method of supporting missionaries, and I'm afraid that I wouldn't be very good at raising money.

4. *I don't know if I have the gift of evangelism.* I hear that either you have the gift or you don't, and that's all there is to it. I'm afraid to admit it, but I've never led anyone to Christ even here at home.

5. *I don't know what would happen to my chances for a career or marriage if I became a missionary overseas.* I'm not getting any younger. I wonder if I'd be doing the right thing by leaving behind so many marriageable people of my own age and religious convictions. And what would happen to my chances to build up tenure in a business or profession—or to qualify for a suitable pension at retirement? I'm afraid that I'd better stay put and leave missionary work to somebody else.

6. *I don't know how safe it is anymore to go into foreign missions.* From what I hear, Christians in many countries face opposition, persecution—or, even worse, bodily harm or death. Frankly, such prospects make me afraid even to consider missionary service.

7. *Coming right down to basics, I don't know if I have a call to mission service.* My pastor tells me that's one thing I must be convinced about—or I should forget about my responsibility to bring the gospel to unreached people. After all, I can pray for the unsaved multitudes without leaving home. I'm afraid that there's not much more I can do about missions—unless I get the call.

Some of the foregoing comments are purely imaginary, to be sure. But at least some potential candidates are sidelined by the "fear factor."

Responding to the Fear Factor

What should be said to fellow Christians who are afraid to commit themselves to vocations in world missions at home and abroad?

Probably the first help that can be given to such Christians is for us to agree that fear of the unknown is understandable. A person usually is somewhat afraid on the night before he or she is to undergo major surgery. On the night before a major battle a soldier is entitled to a serious case of the jitters. Even college students on the night before final exams are known to exhibit symptoms of a strange malady described by some as "cramitis transitorius."

Adjustments

It is helpful to identify objectively with a person's rational fears concerning missionary service. It is a major adjustment for anyone to exchange close family ties for occasional overseas telephone calls, monthly letters, and visits home once in two or three years. One certainly can become lonely, at least until or unless new friends can be found among fellow believers in another part of the world.

Language learning and cultural adjustment do not come quickly for many new missionaries. Gradually, however, one discovers with delight that the strangeness of a new environment fades, that interest in others helps in making friends, and that a willingness to laugh at one's own mistakes in stammering a new language goes a long way toward learning it.

Finances

The fears about raising financial support are understandable, too. In an ideal Christian world, churches would be eager to support missionaries and all other Christian workers with an appropriate salary. And, happily, some churches and denominations do provide salaries for pastors, Christian education workers, evangelists, and missionaries.

But when it comes to financial support for missionaries around the world, we find that about nine out of ten receive no fixed salaries. Must the Lord's work be curtailed as a consequence? Or must those who work for the progress of the gospel look to God to supply their needs in another way?

By faith, members of China Inland Mission—almost one thousand of them at a peak worker force about one century ago—saw God supply funds as they worked to evangelize mainland China. Today, about six thousand members of Wycliffe Bible Translators working in countries around the world look by faith to the Lord to supply their support needs—and they have not found him unable or unwilling to do so. Tens of thousands of additional workers, serving with numerous mission agencies, are supported in the same way as the Lord provides funds through the fellowship of his people. Personally, I testify also that during more than twenty-three years of conducting missionary training programs in Mexico I knew of no qualified applicant who had to stay home for lack of funds.

Those who hesitate to enter missionary service because of financial concerns might adopt a viewpoint broader than money alone. If God has provided a potential worker with good health, has enabled him or her to complete academic studies satisfactorily, has opened the way to the endorsement and prayers of the church, and has given the applicant the desire to help spread the gospel, is he not able also to provide funds for the applicant's support?

Many of us have fears about involvement in evangelism or personal witnessing. Thank God for the local churches which provide ongoing opportunities for evangelistic training and ministry for their members! Thank God for other programs of study and practical evangelistic experience for Christians. Such training not only helps to remove fears about sharing the Lord Jesus with others, it also introduces us to the joys of witnessing for Christ.

Even limited experience in personal witnessing reveals another secret: Personal evangelism usually takes place as the result of Christians' interest, care, and love for other people—especially in times of need. Witnessing is more a matter of friendliness than formula! The Lord brings us into other people's lives as we live close to him and pray for him to lead. Gradually, our fear of witnessing to others about the Lord Jesus will diminish or disappear.

Singleness

What about the apprehension that long-term missionary service may deprive a person of opportunities for Christian marriage or for financial security during retirement as well as working years?

We must ask the Lord for wisdom to help us view our fears about material needs from the perspective of his Word. He is fully as able to provide for our temporal well-being while we devote ourselves to the progress of the gospel as when we work for a less important employer! Further, it may come as a surprise for many Christians to know how adequately most mission boards today have set up the support package for missionaries and their families—including medical and surgical insurance, marriage and child allowances, savings plan, and retirement fund.

The fears about marriage opportunities touch a tender spot—the heart. The yearning for a marriage partner is God-given, and often he fills that yearning by providing for the Christian a spouse of like precious faith.

At the same time, as the years pass, a Christian may realize that the Lord may be leading him or her to singleness instead of marriage. If such be the case, single persons who love Christ may find greater significance and fulfillment in working for the progress of the gospel than in continuing to work in their home communities. The company of like-minded missionary friends can be fully as meaningful and rewarding as the fellowship of Christian friends at home.

And then there are the surprises which God springs on Christian singles in missionary service. Sometimes he delights to bring together single men and women who have the same faith, the same concern for the spread of the gospel, and similar experiences of God's guidance and provision. Many happy marriages have come about on the mission field in this way.

An example of God's providence comes from Central America. A twenty-six-year-old participant in a Mexico Summer Training Session offered herself for a one-year mission assignment after the summer program ended. During her year of service as a missionary teacher in a Central American country, she met a single young man who had completed almost a decade of cross-cultural Christian service.

My wife and I were delighted when we heard from the young lady: "Guess what! This young man and I have been dating since the first of January." The young couple went on to announce their engagement, and subsequently they married. Wonders never cease to happen—even among singles who offer themselves for mission service far from home.

Suffering

Then there is the fear about possible hardship which a missionary may experience as a result of being identified as a follower of Jesus Christ in an area where people are hostile to Christ.

This is a serious issue. In an age of terrorism and hostage taking, hostile religious fanaticism may bring sudden injury, death, or captivity to missionaries as well as to other Christians. Every one of us must come to terms with this possibility, especially when we follow Christ to serve him outside North America and Europe.

Consider the facts in the matter of persecution against Christians. David Barrett and his research staff have tried to trace the persistence of persecution through the centuries. They come to the surprising conclusion that persecution and martyrdom have increased from one century to the next—until the number of actual martyrs for the sake of Christ in the twentieth century may exceed all centuries before it!

Hostility to Christ and his people often is encountered in Muslim lands. Even in a country such as Turkey—a member of NATO and considered a Western-style democracy with constitutional guarantees of religious freedom—persecution of Christians is not uncommon.

The February 1990 issue of *Missionary Monthly* published a letter from Turkey. It was titled, "A Cry from a Turkish Believer," and it read in part:

Presently I am studying in the university. . . . The university where I am studying is situated in a very extremely Islamic city of Turkey. There is unbelievable oppression and torture against those who don't yield to Islamic precepts. . . .

One night the police raided my room. They beat me and carried me away. The [Christian] books you sent me were in my jacket pocket. For days I was interrogated and systematically tortured. They excreted on my books and forced me to eat their excrement. The beatings did not move me, but the insults they made on my Jesus and my religion were worse than death to me. . . .

The policemen, . . . who could not stand my having found the truth, informed the university professors. . . . Even though I study diligently, all teachers have taken a stand against me and give me low grades. . . . [One of the professors] doesn't even let me into the class. Whenever I attempt to get in, he rebukes me, saying, "Scram, you dirty Christian bastard!"

Also in February 1990, the Latin America Mission's office staff in Miami, Florida, released news of persecution experienced by evangelicals in Mexico. Under the caption, "Evangelical Christians Attacked in Mexico City During All-Night Prayer Meeting; Chased like Animals," the news release read:

Mexico City, Monday, February 5—A mob of fanatical Roman Catholics estimated at 10,000 people attacked and chased a group of 160 evangelical Christians around midnight on February 2 in the Ajusco area of Mexico City, where the evangelicals had gone to hold an all-night open-air meeting to intercede for the salvation of the city. . . .

> Humanly speaking, the evangelicals credit Mexican law enforcement personnel with saving their lives. Ten squad cars arrived at the scene soon after the attack reached its strongest point and helped protect them as they fled. . . . Seven ambulances also arrived.
>
> The three leaders of the evangelical group, all mature pastors [including Juan M. Isais], were beaten badly. . . . In some cases, four or five men pursued young women with rocks and machetes. . . .
>
> Juan Isais, who identified himself as leader of the prayer meeting, was told: "We are believers in Jesus Christ; we belong to the virgin of Guadalupe and we do not want you here. Get out before we kill you; we are the authority here!"

The warning of the Lord Jesus to his disciples is still true: "In the world you shall have tribulation." Think of those who have suffered and died for Christ in the last half century alone—in China, in the Soviet Union during its most repressive years, in Muslim lands, in Latin America and elsewhere.

But Jesus also said: "But be of good cheer: I have overcome the world" (John 16:33 KJV). How can we be at peace, how can we be of good cheer when suffering and persecution continue to face those who love the Lord Jesus? How can we be anything but afraid under such circumstances and hesitate to go as missionaries into such a hostile world?

God provides three cardinal consolations concerning Christian suffering and persecution. One is that suffering is a gift from God by which those who suffer for Christ come to know him more intimately. Read Philippians 1:29 and 3:10 where Paul expresses his desire to know Christ, the fellowship of his sufferings, and the power of his resurrection.

Another consolation from God is that in enduring suffering for Christ without continual complaint, the believer finds his or her witness is made unusually effective by the Holy

Spirit. Reports about the witness of believers imprisoned during China's Cultural Revolution tell about many Communist cadre members, prison guards, and prisoners being brought to Christ. God was pleased to accomplish all this through the witness of confined and tortured Christians.

The apostle Paul had the same experience during his confinement at Rome. In Philippians 1:12 he reported, "What has happened to me has really served to advance the gospel." Strange as it may seem, the church often is most healthy and grows most rapidly where it lives under constant pressure and persecution. What is God saying to his church by this today?

The supreme consolation for persecuted Christians rests in God's assurance that if we are faithful to death we will receive a "crown of life" (Revelation 2:10). That is why Paul could say with optimism, "I consider that our present sufferings are not worth comparing with the glory that will be revealed in us" (Romans 8:18).

This is not to say that our fears of persecution and death can be rationalized away, even by quoting texts from the Word of God. What we bear witness to is this: The answer to our fears is available. It comes by grace as a gift from God to those who believe what he promises in his Word. Even if many of Christ's disciples must become martyrs, the lesson of history is summed up in the saying from ancient times that "the blood of martyrs is the seed of the church."

The Missionary Call

One other cause of reluctance for Christians about entering a missionary vocation is the fear that a person does not have a special call from God for such work. Without attempting to answer this anxiety too hastily, consider a question which gets to the bottom line of this hesitation. If Jesus includes the entire church in his call to "disciple all the peoples," what other call to mission does anyone need? Two-thirds of the world's people are lost apart from Christ. With the majority of them living far from where we live, would not you and I need a special call from the Lord *to stay home,* instead of a special call *to go?*

Move Out of Your Fears

Among the many things of which we honestly may be afraid, one may be the prospect of missionary service—short-term as well as long-term.

It is not shameful to be afraid. But it is a shame to keep our fears to ourselves—particularly when the Lord is willing and able to relieve us of them. David said, "What time I am afraid, I will trust in Thee" (Psalm 56:3 KJV). Good counsel! The psalm writer also reported, "I sought the LORD, and he answered me; he delivered me from all my fears" (Psalm 34:4).

You may have been hesitating about making a commitment to missionary service. It may not necessarily be that something is spiritually wrong with your heart, eyes, head, knees, or ears—problems about which President McQuilkin wrote in *The Great Omission.* The main cause of your hesitation and reluctance may be fear.

Move out of your fears. Hand them over to the Lord. Christ will set you free from fear as you put your trust in him. He calls you to serve him in the mission of his church, and as he calls, he tells you not to be afraid. "Therefore, go and make disciples of all nations . . . and surely I am with you always . . ." (Matthew 28:19–20).

4

Become God's Person

Thea

We call our world today a "global village." Television, fax machines, satellites, and jet travel keep us in touch with every part of the earth, just as people in a small village know what is happening to each of their neighbors.

On our TV screens we have seen, within hours of the events, Chinese students occupying Tiananmen Square, Berliners pouring through the breached wall, Israeli soldiers chasing Palestinians in Nablus, Jesuit priests lying bullet-ridden in their El Salvador garden, Hungarians streaming forward at a Billy Graham rally in Budapest, and South Africans celebrating the release of Nelson Mandela from prison. From the safety of our sofas, we watch volcanos erupt, earthquakes shudder, fires rage, floods swallow, and oil spills destroy. The sights and sounds of the whole world are as close as the buttons on our remote controls.

Not as easily flicked on and off are the people from other parts of the global village who have arrived in our communities. They are flesh and blood strangers looking for ways to survive, to be accepted. Colleges and universities have overseas students and exchange professors. Refugees from Vietnam and Cambodia are clustering in such unlikely places as Wisconsin and Ontario. Toronto is a small United Nations, and by the year 2000 the population of Los Angeles will be predominantly Hispanic and Asian. In California one may choose from six languages in which to take a driver's test. Spanish has become the primary language for much of Florida and Texas. Signs in Miami store windows which formerly said, "*Se habla español*" now say, "English spoken here," as if English is the exception.

God is stirring up an incredible mix of people on our planet. American waste management people are in Saudi Arabia, Turkish workers find employment in Germany, and Japanese are in the States and Canada supervising businesses they have purchased. A man from Hong Kong bought the Vancouver site of a world's fair, and Russian trainees were in the Chicago area learning how to be efficient and friendly for the huge McDonald's in Moscow. Hostages from the West sit for years with their Shiite Muslim captors in Lebanon, while Western businessmen are rushing into the newly open countries of Eastern Europe. American military personnel, for better or for worse, are all over the world, and the prisons of every country hold people of other nationalities.

A Challenge to Cross-cultural Ministry

In this kind of world I challenge you to be part of cross-cultural ministry, far away and near home. Cross-cultural ministry means reaching out to people who have grown up learning values and living patterns different from our own. Cross-cultural ministry begins with an attitude of seeking such people, having our "radar" out to help them and introduce them to Jesus.

I challenge you to cross-cultural ministry for four reasons:

1. Here, in cross-cultural settings, are the greatest needs and the fewest workers in the task God has given us to do. Here are concentrations of the Christ-less, the poor and helpless, the left out and transplanted, the unreached people, near at hand and especially in parts of our global village where no Christians live.
2. You are the young and flexible generation. You are at a point in life where you are seeking God's guidance, exploring needs, making choices. You do not have the encumbrances of established homes and entrenched business responsibilities; you have not settled down somewhere to stay. You have the vitality and vision to take on new challenges, and you want to serve where God needs you most. His kingdom encompasses the whole world, not just the culture in which you grew up.
3. You have had good preparation. Many of you come from strong Christian homes and churches. You have attended Christian colleges which teach and apply the Bible thoroughly, or you have grappled with what a Christian believes and does in the milieu of a secular university where your relationship to Christ was tested and deepened. You have a

sound foundation for ministry, and you are prepared to build on it.

4. Above all, there is greater reward and joy in seeing
Christ change the lives of others than in living just
to protect and enhance your own. When we move
out of our well-padded Christian ruts to serve in
different areas of God's growing family, *we* are the
ones who are blessed as we share in the big picture
of God's working and certain victory. People are the
only earthly "things" we can take along to heaven,
and we need to concentrate on helping them find
the way to live and die happily.

I am impressed with how many people of my retirement
age look back on lives spent becoming materially successful
and secure and now say, "If I could do it over again, I would
use my time for people and the things that really matter." I
confess to some of those thoughts, too. But none of us who
are older can roll back the clock. You are the ones with life
ahead of you. Choose well the first time because there is no
second go-round. Paul said to the Corinthians, "So we fix
our eyes not on what is seen, but on what is unseen. For
what is seen is temporary, but what is unseen is eternal"
(2 Corinthians 4:18).

What Kind of Person Does God Use?

With this challenge and introduction, let's talk about the
kind of person God uses in cross-cultural ministry. In the
next chapter we will look at relationships in cross-cultural
ministry. I believe that the persons we are and the relationships we make are the greatest human resources of our part-

nership with Christ in establishing his kingdom. After all, the Christian life is persons living in relationship—Christ's to us, and ours to him and to one another.

What kind of person does God use for cross-cultural ministry, for reaching people who have different values and living patterns than our own?

A Person Close to Christ

God uses people who are in living relationship to his Son, who has saved us and is remodeling us through his Spirit to be more like him. Do we need to talk in a Bible college about a personal relationship to Jesus Christ? Christian colleges and seminaries can be both wonderful and frightening: Students may be so busy analyzing doctrines and memorizing outlines that they miss the person of Jesus Christ and the power of his Spirit. "I was so overwhelmed taking tests and writing papers about religious things that I had no time for my personal walk with the Lord," a young pastor told me. "I came out of seminary farther from the Lord than when I entered it."

The desire to be in ministry for Christ flows out of a deep enabling relationship to him as Savior and Lord. Without that, anything we do is hollow, even though we become adept at going through the motions. Paul, the incomparable cross-cultural missionary, wrote the Colossians, "This is my work and I can do it only because Christ's mighty energy is at work within me" (Colossians 1:29 LB). Cross-cultural ministry lives and grows out of our relationship to Jesus Christ. As we hear him and speak with him in daily quiet time, we will grow through obedience to be more like him.

A Person Channeling God's Gifts

In Christ's relationship to us he gives many gifts which change and empower our lives. We then become human channels of these gifts to others, and this is our ministry of love to them. There are four gifts which I believe have special application to a person in cross-cultural ministry.

The gift of unconditional love

"While we were still sinners," God loved us so astoundingly that he had his only child killed for us. God didn't wait for us to clean up our act, to look more presentable, or to concoct our own scheme for getting back into his favor. God loved us *as* we were and *where* we were. He came looking for us like Christ's parable shepherd seeking his lost sheep.

Have you ever been in love, or thought you were? Did you worry that the person you loved might not love you just as you were? If she really knew me, she wouldn't love me, you thought. Well, God really knew us in our helpless, hopeless sin, and he really did love us unconditionally as we were.

God gives us his unconditional love to pass on to others. People are longing for that kind of love, but it is rare and they find it hard to believe. When our daughter Tess and her partner, who work in literacy with Wycliffe Bible Translators, went to their first Quechua village high in the mountains of Peru, they were viewed with suspicion. Later they learned what the townspeople thought when they first arrived. "They are looking for gold in the river," said some. "They pretend to be kind, but they are sly inside and might kidnap our children to sell them," said others. "Why would they come from their rich country to learn our language unless they plan to sell our words for money when they go home?"

In Muslim countries it is often the steady, unbelievable love of Christians which breaks through the barriers, because Islam is a revengeful religion which does not meet the human heart cry for unconditional love. People cannot imagine there is such love for free, even though they long for it because God has made them restless for him.

We find it hard to give that unconditional love, especially to people who are different from us. They take us out of our comfort zone; they make us uneasy, insecure, and we prefer to ignore them. For example, I do not know how to relate to a bitter street kid who trusts no one. I feel humiliated trying to speak Spanish in Mexico so I dislike being there.

It is easier to criticize, to look down on someone, and to make an excuse for turning away. I remember a college student who used to do that about rich people. Often and loudly Jim proclaimed that no rich person could be a Christian. Was that his way of disposing of people with whom he was uncomfortable?

We need the resources of God's unfailing love to become persons reaching out to people different from ourselves, and we need to practice the obedience of loving. Henri Nouwen calls it "creating free and friendly space for strangers." It's like taking someone we find difficult to love into the safe, quiet capsule of Christ's love, from which both of us can reenter the painful world around us.

Paul wrote to the Ephesians, "I pray that you, being rooted and established in love, may have power, together with all the saints, to grasp how wide and long and high and deep is the love of Christ, and to know this love that surpasses knowledge" (Ephesians 3:17–19). We have "the glorious riches" of that love for cross-cultural ministry. It replaces our reluctance and dislikes. It is the greatest gift we can channel to others as a sample of the boundless love God offers them.

God uses in cross-cultural ministry a person who practices the unconditional love of Christ.

The gift of forgiveness

God forgives and accepts us so that we may be both forgiven and forgiving.

God has every right not to forgive our big and little rebellions against him. But when we confess our sin, he forgives us completely in his Son and chooses not to remember what we have done against him. His is an attitude of forgiveness, like that of the father who ran down the road to meet his prodigal son. In the same way, Jesus when he was crucified and Stephen when he was stoned asked the Father to forgive their murderers even though there is no record that the murderers were asking to be forgiven.

"If you do not forgive men their sins, your Father will not forgive your sins," Jesus tells us in the Sermon on the Mount (Matthew 6:15). How often, Lord, must we do this? "Seventy times seven," he replies, using numbers of infinity. On our own we cannot forgive. We naturally go on blaming, taking offense, coddling our bitternesses toward others. Only God's gift of forgiveness delivers us and makes it possible for us to forgive and accept others, so that they may know what it means to be totally forgiven and accepted by God.

Corrie ten Boom offered forgiveness to her cruel concentration camp guard when she met him after World War II was over. Elisabeth Elliot forgave the Auca Indians who killed her husband and four other missionaries; later she herself brought the gospel to this unreached tribe. An inner-city worker forgives the addict he befriended who robbed him of all his possessions. A mother forgives her son's murderer and visits him during his years in prison.

People without Christ are surprised and dumbfounded by the forgiveness of God channeled through us in this world of long hatreds and sudden flareups. Evangelist Luis Palau, preaching recently in the Soviet Union, reports that it was the message of God's full forgiveness which most moved his audiences.

God uses in cross-cultural ministry persons who have been changed by his amazing forgiveness and who demonstrate an attitude of forgiveness and acceptance in all their relationships.

The gift of Jesus' model

Christ, more than anyone, entered cross-cultural ministry! Leaving his supreme position in a perfect heaven, he became fully human on a miserable planet. He entered there a helpless baby and was willing to learn humbly from infancy on. For thirty years the Son of God was known as a carpenter's obedient son in a village on the "wrong side of the tracks," living inconspicuously with the people he had come to save. In his adopted culture he followed a simple lifestyle with no house of his own and unencumbered by material things.

Jesus sought out people whom others avoided: the poor, lepers, prostitutes, the handicapped, and widows. Common people were important to him, but he put the status-hungry Pharisees in their place.

In Mexico there lives a capable young Indian pastor. Often when he leaves his tribe to do business in a large city he is the victim of subtle discrimination. In a store others may be waited on ahead of him, or he is treated discourteously at a hotel desk. One evening a missionary in whose courtyard we had held a Bible study complained that one of his folding chairs was missing. "I'll bet that Indian took it," he said. "I don't trust him around here." Wouldn't Jesus have rebuked that missionary?

Try to imagine how and where Jesus would live if he came into our world today. How counter-culture he would be, emptying himself to be a servant among people whose goals are security, success, and wealth!

Christ, in his lifestyle and values also shows us how to suffer for him. In fact, he makes it sound as if this is a normal result of our choice to "take up your cross and follow me." Paul says, "The sufferings of Christ flow over into our lives. . . . For we who are alive are always being given over to death for Jesus' sake, so that his life may be revealed in our mortal body" (2 Corinthians 1:5 and 4:11).

Dr. Helen Roseveare told an Urbana missionary conference about her sufferings in the then Belgian Congo. In the agony of her rapings and beatings she remembered that Jesus had suffered far more for her. "So why should I have been excused from suffering for him?" she asked with glowing face. Stephen's face was radiant, too, when he was stoned to death.

At the 1989 Lausanne II Conference on World Evangelization in Manila, everyone was moved by the testimony of a Chinese pastor imprisoned by a Communist regime for seventeen years. His prison job was to gather human waste from the cells and tend it in the dung pit from which it would be taken to fertilize the fields. Since no one came near this stinking pit, Chen Min Yen used the privacy to sing and pray as loudly as he wished. His favorite song was a Chinese translation of an old English hymn, "In the Garden." As he had sung in his dung pit garden, he sang unaccompanied to the 4,000 Lausanne delegates, "I come to the garden alone . . . and he walks with me and he talks with me and he tells me I am his own." Today Chen goes in and out of mainland China from Hong Kong, tirelessly teaching and strengthening believers in the underground churches.

Christ's earthly model to us includes the model of suffering. Though I shrink from it, I see in those who have suffered for Christ the glow and power of a life refined by fire. I am only learning not to complain about gnat bites and humid heat and warm pop and bucket flushing during our annual primitive student camp in Mexico!

All of us are accountable to God to apply Christ's earthly model to the way we live. We should not criticize one another for how each of us chooses to follow it. But we wealthy Americans from a powerful country have a heavy responsibility to radically rethink how to imitate the model of Christ as he became cross-cultural for us.

God uniquely uses in cross-cultural ministry persons who are willing to identify with the earthly values, lifestyle, and even suffering of Christ.

The gift of God's trustworthiness

God promises us the security of trusting him to be in total control of every person and every happening in this world. He will "get it all together." He is working out everything everywhere in all centuries for good and for his glory. Jesus sits at God's right hand with all power given to him. The Holy Spirit is at work everywhere, and all the angels have their orders. So we can, we must, give up worrying about the results of our efforts. We must quit trying to make certain things happen. We must stop wanting to be in control and give up being impatient with others for what they do or do not do. It is *out* of our hands and *into* God's.

What relief and freedom to leave the when and how of everything to God!

Sometimes God shows us his plan clearly. At Manila's Lausanne II conference it was overwhelming to see Christians from 270 countries gathered as abundant proof that God is bringing in his family from every tribe and tongue and nation.

Sometimes God's plan is hidden. Who could have dreamed that behind the bamboo curtain without Bibles, churches, pastors, or missionaries, God was bringing fifty million Chinese people to faith in his Son?

Sometimes God's plan seems to take a long time. Two men attended the funeral of an old friend who had become a Christian in the last months of his life. "Isn't it great that John finally came to the Lord!" said one. "Yes," replied the other. "I prayed for him for thirty-seven years." For decades Christians have been praying for a breakthrough in the large Muslim world, and now there is talk of "the dawn before the dawn."

Sometimes God's plans are to bring good out of heartbreak. Jacob lost his favorite son for more than twenty years so that all his descendants could be kept from starvation. "You meant it for evil but God used it for good," Joseph told his frightened brothers. Chet Bitterman of Wycliffe was killed by terrorists in Colombia, and three hundred young people subsequently volunteered to take his place on mission fields of the world. Only God can use for good all the bad and painful things that sin has brought into our world. Every mission field and ministry has true stories to prove that God is incredible and full of surprises in his trustworthiness.

He is trustworthy even when his plans drive us to him in utter helplessness, pleading because everything seems wrong and there is no glimpse of light at the end of the tunnel. A little poem I received from a friend says it this way:

> Trust him when dark doubts assail you,
> Trust him when your strength is small.
> Trust him when to only trust him
> Is the hardest thing of all.

On the bulletin board above my desk is my favorite cartoon. A pastor is sitting in his study at his desk on which stands a metal organizer for his work. The bottom basket says "Out" and the next basket is labeled "In." Then there is a third basket which is marked "Up." One of God's greatest gifts to those who work with him is his "Up" basket. He gives us the freedom to keep on doing our part, leaving the results to him. He teaches us to trust that he has made and is carrying out his perfect master plan.

In the strangeness and seeming setbacks of cross-cultural ministry, the gift of God's "Up" basket is priceless. Paul knew this when he encouraged the Christians in Rome: "May the God of hope fill you with all joy and peace as you trust in him" (Romans 15:13a).

God uses in cross-cultural ministry persons who are learning, often through struggle, to persevere while claiming the absolute trustworthiness of their Father in heaven.

Becoming God's Person

What kind of persons does God use in cross-cultural ministry? He uses those who live in close relationship to his Son, who receive special gifts through the Spirit to use in ministry to others. Among these gifts are God's unconditional love, full forgiveness in Christ and the grace to be forgiving, the counter-cultural model of Jesus' life on earth, and the mighty trustworthiness of God to complete his perfect plan for the world and its people.

God does not give us his gifts neatly tied in pretty wrappings. Nor does he press a button to produce an instant cross-cultural co-worker. He "grows" us into persons he uses. The process of our growing in receiving and channeling his gifts is more important to him than any other achievement of our lives. He is more concerned with what we become than with what we accomplish.

Neither does God drag us kicking and screaming to places we do not want to go. However the mystery is explained of our freedom to choose and God's eternal plan, one thing is certain: God and his Word are true and trustworthy. His promises are guaranteed in Christ and confirmed by the Holy Spirit in our minds and hearts. Our part is to believe, obey, and trust him.

As God continues his process of growth in us, he makes us ready and glad to serve him, even in the challenges of cross-cultural ministry.

5

Build Christ-like Relationships

Thea

Living in Relationships

It was God's idea that people should live in relationships. He himself lives relationally in the perfect Trinity of Father, Son, and Spirit. When God created man in his image, he made Eve because it was not good for Adam to be alone. So God placed Adam and Eve in relationship to him and to one another, and every baby born into the world since then has also entered those two relationships. Sin has done terrible things to our relationships, but it cannot take away the longing God created in us to be in loving connection to him and to one another.

The Bible can be called a book about relationships. In it God unfolds his amazing plan to restore our relationship to him through his Son. He gives endless examples of how

people related to him and to one another in godly and
ungodly ways, and he clearly teaches how he wants us to live.
Jesus' summary of the commandments is relational—love
God above all and love your neighbor as yourself.

I am a social worker, not a theologian or missiologist. I
like to think of evangelism and ministry as the "show-and-
tell" of how God restores our relationship to him and to
one another. If we can't show that God's saving love
changes our lives, how can we recommend him to others?
That's why relationships are so important in Christian ministry, especially in the challenges of cultures different from
our own.

Doing Our Homework

God established our earthly relationships by putting us
in families. There are many kinds of families, none of them
perfect in this sin-filled world. What happens in our families has a powerful effect on us; these primary relationships
bring the most intense joy and pain of our lives.

Growing up to be God's person means that I take my
responsibility to love my parents and siblings as God loves
me, no matter what has happened or is happening in my
family. I give up blaming and anger, I forgive freely as
Christ forgave me, and I ask forgiveness for my part in any
estrangement. Then I pray and trust God to work in the
lives of my family members according to his timing and
process. Too hard, you say? Never sell the Holy Spirit
short!

Many of us have old hurts and unfinished business with
family members. One sad result is that these unresolved
feelings and relationships piggyback along with us, cloud-
ing and hampering the way we relate to others, also in
ministry. God intends our families to be the primary work-

shop for relationships. If we do our basic love and reconciliation homework there, we will be free to make other mature relationships also.

God adopts us into a larger Christian family in the churches we attend. There are many kinds of churches and church members, none of them perfect either in this sin-filled world.

God intends churches to be centers for worshiping and learning from him, for loving and encouraging one another, and for reaching out to "show-and-tell" his love to others. But often our church relationships become argumentative, grudging, competitive. We spend our energies criticizing and labeling each other when instead we should be "Speaking the truth in love" (Ephesians 4:15). Satan must be delighted to keep us bickering among ourselves while God's love and Good News go undemonstrated and unshared.

Sometimes it may be hard for you to find your place in the church. It is easier to blame, criticize, and keep your distance. But God means for you to take your responsibility in this imperfect family, too. Ask him to give you his unconditional love for your church family, and be at peace trusting him to work out whatever plans he has for it. Then find some class or program in your church which majors in reaching out, and do your part in it inconspicuously but with all your heart.

The relationships that we develop in our families and practice humbly in our churches are the foundation for cross-cultural ties we will make. There will be many new challenges in another culture, but the foundation of Christ's gifts applied in our relationships will be the same wherever we go.

Let me give an example. Many years ago on a moonlit October night a friend and I went canoeing on a wide river. The canoe overturned and we fell into deep water. We retrieved the paddles and stayed with the canoe until friends in another boat helped us reach the shore. Treading water in my woolen slacks, I was thankful that I had learned to swim well just a few years earlier. Even though we were in an uncertain situation, I was not helpless and paralyzed by fear.

That's how it is when we face the strangeness of cross-cultural relationships equipped with the experience of Christ-like relationships already established in our families and churches. I urge you to do that homework now. God asks us to do it anyway, to love our home and church families as he loves us.

The Biggest Problem

What happens in our relationships when we enter a new cultural setting? Though we may be committed to following Christ's earthly model, we are often unprepared for our feelings while being reduced from capable functioning adults to helpless learning children. We know neither the language and customs, nor how to find the things we need. In the beginning, even if we figure out how to ask a question, we may not understand the answer! We feel isolated, useless, and put down.

In our frustration, we may turn against the people closest to us, fellow workers from our own culture. We envy their abilities and progress. Unconsciously, perhaps, we try to cut them down. In the process of working together, we want others to follow our ways and ideas or we block them from achieving theirs. We do not work and pray for unity, nor do we have the grace to rejoice in the talents of others.

All around the world there are cross-cultural ministries plagued by bad relationships between Christian workers. This is probably the biggest problem on mission fields. If we cannot love and work with our own people, why should those to whom we witness trust us to love and work with them? Why should they trust the Savior whom we come to share?

In the Mexican state of Oaxaca there were four ministry couples who disagreed and talked behind each others' backs. After months of friction and mistrust, they were convicted of their behavior. Confessing to God and to each other, they made a covenant to communicate directly and lovingly. The Lord blessed their new beginning. Be assured that God is able and ready to help us face the unexpected problems of relationships with fellow workers and to restore us to the unity and love we have in Christ as we serve him in unfamiliar settings.

Relationships, learned and remodeled in the family and developed in the church at home, can be strengthened and purified with fellow workers in new cultures. Then we are ready to relate to people whose lifestyles and values are different from our own.

Sharing Our Lives

Paul told the Thessalonians, "We loved you so much that we were delighted to share with you not only the gospel of God but our lives as well" (1 Thessalonians 2:8). "Sharing our lives" means learning to understand and respect how our new brothers and sisters live, adapting our ways to their patterns of thinking and doing. Above all, while we make many blunders, we are to share our lives by taking on the attitude of Christ, who "made himself nothing, taking the very nature of a servant" (Philippians 2:7).

But we are so ingrained in our own ways that we do not realize how hard it is to see things another way, and how crucial it is to develop relationships on the basis of respecting and adapting to another lifestyle.

Let's look at some examples of differences in lifestyles and values.

How Late Is Late?

If you agree on a time to meet a friend for lunch, how long will you wait before you feel irritated? One study shows that North Americans excuse someone up to five minutes late. We get tense after waiting fifteen minutes and angry after half an hour. But Latin Americans expect people to be at least half an hour late. In fact, they are surprised if a guest arrives on time. They do not become tense until an hour has passed and they become upset only after two hours.

A few years ago a young man from Michigan married a young Mexican lady in Merida, Mexico. Their invitations listed the wedding time as 3:00 P.M. They planned to begin the ceremony at four o'clock, hoping that the last of their guests would have arrived by then. The couple told the officiating missionary that the wedding would begin at 4:00 P.M., assuming he would think like a North American. When the day came and the missionary saw 4:00 P.M. in his datebook, he assumed it was Mexican time and arrived at the church close to 5:00 P.M. By that time the ceremony was over. Another pastor in the audience had performed it.

Time means different things in different cultures. Most North Americans are controlled by time. We live by a schedule with punctual beginnings and endings. But most non-Westerners see an event and the people involved as more important than the time. Whatever is happening deserves to take as long as necessary to include everyone and everything. Occasions begin when the last person arrives and have no planned cutoff time.

My friend Kitty Miller wrote a case study thesis on whether a literacy program in Papua New Guinea fit the needs of the local people being trained as teachers. She observed that the Western pattern of timed class periods cut off student response abruptly at the end of a class hour and made the students reluctant to begin a discussion they could not complete.

Similarly, while Americans begin to squirm if a church service lasts beyond an hour, non-Western services begin when everyone and everything is ready and may continue for several hours.

We have learned in Mexico that a promise to do something *mañana* does not really mean *tomorrow*. It simply means *not today*. It might not be done tomorrow either! I am organized by lists and schedules and my husband is doubly organized! How hard it is when we come to an event-oriented culture to humbly honor that way of life in our relationships, and to appreciate its good points, even if we continue our scheduled ways in private.

People Versus Paper

In 1980 my husband and I went to Pattaya, Thailand, for an international gathering of Christian workers to discuss world evangelization. The hundreds of delegates were divided into working groups for the first five days, with each group assigned to prepare a written report for presentation to the whole body. Each group had a typist; I agreed to type for the Latin Americans.

However, after four days of Latin American group meetings there was no sign of anything to type. These brothers and sisters from various Latin countries were sharing photos of their families and ministries, singing and praying together, reporting and rejoicing in what the Lord had done for each of them. They had an inspiring time and forged strong bonds. Then, with the deadline almost upon them, three members of the group (one an "organized" Scottish missionary) stayed up most of one night drafting a report which the group approved the fifth day and I typed most of the fifth night.

This was no problem to the Latin Americans; the time they had spent together and the relationships established were more valuable than the report. Reports gather dust on a shelf, while what happens between people is lasting. But we North Americans come from a culture which writes reports, keeps records, establishes goals, and evaluates progress. Imagine how we look to another culture, completing paperwork for an office on the other side of the world while the needy stand waiting at our windows.

The Individual and the Group

Most of us have grown up in a culture which increasingly defends the right of a person to make choices and seek satisfactions with little consideration of what this does to others. Individual rights are paramount. In most cultures of the world this is not so.

On an island in the Pacific a missionary invited some young people to learn to play croquet on his lawn. One of the guests learned quickly and was well ahead of the others. But he deliberately kept hitting his ball off course. To the missionary's amazement, the winning man was waiting for the others to catch up so that the group could finish together. In that culture, and in many others, it is shameful to stand out as an individual and to achieve apart from the group. The achiever may be ridiculed and ostracized for making others look less able. Western competition makes these people very uncomfortable.

When the Christian Quechua Indians of Peru gather twice a year for music festivals, each church prepares a singing group. People travel on foot for days to participate. But there is no thought of judging which groups are best. One year an insensitive missionary suggested awarding prizes for the finest performances. The response was silent embarrassment.

A young missionary couple in an African country was having an argument. Their voices carried through the open windows of their small home. That evening an African elder came to them to say he would work with them until their disagreement was resolved, because the whole compound was responsible to see that the two of them came to peace. The group exercised leadership over the individuals.

In some cultures the group enforces its control over the individual. In Muslim countries the group ostracizes and sometimes kills individuals who convert to Christianity. In southern Mexico there is a new town called Betania built by Christian Chamula Indians forced from their homes by their own tribespeople. Earlier leaders of this tribe once crucified a seventeen-year-old boy of their own group so they would have their own Jesus and not be polluted by outside religions.

In 1983 I taught counseling for a month in Hong Kong to Chinese Christians who were training to enter mainland China. They, however, taught me to rethink counseling for the Chinese who have protected each other for decades by never revealing information or feelings to each other. Anything shared might be tortured out of someone by Communist party block captains. What someone did not know, he could not be forced to reveal. I became aware that many Chinese Christians have carried burdens of private knowledge and chosen to suffer individually to protect their families and underground churches.

Has our culture become a culture of the individual? We have a responsibility to rethink that. When we enter another culture whose strong emphasis is on the group, we are challenged not only to respect its ways but also to search the Bible for what God teaches us about Christ-like relationships.

Marriage and Family Differences

Cultures differ widely in their marriage and family patterns. Sometimes these are hard to discover because family life goes on behind closed doors. Families are the heart of a culture, and we must be especially sensitive to and respectful of the way they function. In many parts of the world the roles of men and women are very different from what has emerged in the Western world, where Christians are debating intensely what biblical roles should be.

There may be differences in parent-child relationships. In China, for example, a forty-year-old man will not move his wife and children to another city without the consent of his parents. A Nepalese student wife dreaded to return to her country because she would be forced to serve as slave to her mother-in-law. But in the United States Ann Landers unhesitatingly advised a newlywed couple to tell their parents to MYOB—mind your own business—when the parents tried to give advice. In most cultures a person would not dream of bringing shame on his family by his behavior. In the States, however, many young adolescents claim the right to make choices independently, regardless of the effect on those close to them.

In the Western world divorce is prevalent. In Latin cultures there are few divorces but mistresses are a way of life. Muslim countries give men the custody of their children and allow them to abandon a wife by declaring on three different days, "I divorce you."

In many cultures the elderly are honored and included in families. You may see their children and grandchildren carefully helping them get around. In North America, however, the healthy elderly make their own lives while most of the helpless elderly are cared for in nursing homes.

We can learn much from the marriage and family patterns of other cultures. We also will be challenged to find the fine line between becoming part of a new culture and living in ways we believe God desires for *all* cultures. Think of the example of a Christian husband who loves and treats his wife as an equal, or a Christian family which makes each Lord's Day a special day.

There is no witness more powerful than a Christian family humbly entering a new culture to share their lives, also by living out the biblical distinctives God wants for families of all cultures.

No Easy Answers

What happens when cultural differences involve what we consider to be moral values? Have you read Don Richardson's book *Peace Child*? He and his wife went to the unreached Sawi tribe in Irian Jaya. Eagerly he learned the language so that he could tell them the story of Jesus. When the Sawi men heard the story, they were excited, but not about Jesus. To them Judas was the hero, because among the Sawis the supreme achievement was to shower an enemy with gifts and attention until, utterly unsuspecting, he was pounced on and killed. Treachery was the value and Judas the hero.

The definition of stealing also varies from culture to culture. If I leave something unattended, or if I have more than someone thinks I need, is it stealing if someone takes it? There are Muslims who consider non-Muslims to be Allah's gift to them for exploiting in every way possible. In some cultures walls are used to keep possessions from view where anyone has the right to take them.

I remember talking with translators who had entered an unreached tribe in Irian Jaya. Whenever they left their house, the people robbed it. Once the chief's son even made off with a piece of meat being roasted behind the house. Is this what Jesus meant when he said, "If someone takes your cloak, do not stop him from taking your tunic. . . . If anyone takes what belongs to you, do not demand it back" (Luke 6:29–30)?

What about bribes in cultures where they are an assumed part of every transaction? Do we give bribes but not take them? Or is refusing to give them a part of our Christian witness? In situations like these, we need to rethink carefully how Christ would want us to respond. Often there are no easy answers.

If a Crisis Hits

Different cultures have different ways of handling crises, too. Lingenfelter and Mayers, in their excellent book *Ministering Cross-Culturally,* tell about two ways of responding to typhoons on Yap Island in the South Pacific. Whenever the radio reported a typhoon in the area, the U.S. Coast Guard immediately secured its equipment, boarded up windows, and sat tight inside, prepared and waiting. But the Yapese went on about their normal business until a typhoon actually hit their coast. Then they worked frantically to salvage what they could.

After all, the Yapese explained, there are about twenty typhoon warnings every year, but in twelve years only one typhoon has come ashore. So why waste time preparing over and over again for what doesn't happen? It is not necessary to plan and act in advance. If a crisis hits, do the best thing possible at that moment. Can you imagine how hard it is on relationships when people with such varying viewpoints have to live together and share decision making about how to proceed?

How Shall We Worship?

For years most Western missionaries imposed their pattern of worship on the cultures to which they came. Now we are learning to value and encourage whatever form rises from the hearts of believers. What if new Christians pray standing, kneeling, face to the ground, shoes off, hands raised, or all murmuring together at the same time? What kinds of instruments and music will best express their praise of God?

What about the religious patterns of non-Christians in the culture new to us? Should we take part in holy day or feast day customs important to them? Shall we bring food gifts to our Muslim neighbors as they do when the Ramadan fasting month is over? Shall we attend the Bar

Mitvah celebration of a Jewish neighbor's son and invite him to the baptism of our child? Would we celebrate Chinese New Year in Taiwan and Ancestors' Day in Japan? Which are good bridges in our new relationships and which would compromise our Christian witness?

Cues for Daily Living

On my first visit to my husband's Dutch relatives in 1958, they teased me for not smoking with them but they raised their eyebrows at my lipstick. When we were in Spain, Christians served only alcoholic beverages at guest meals because the water was unfit, but in Mexico, where the water is probably worse, no evangelical drinks or smokes as signs of a changed life in a culture where alcohol abuse wrecks many families.

There are differences in daily living patterns which we need to learn, respect, and often adopt. In Muslim culture one does not sit with crossed legs because the bottom of the foot or shoe is dirty, improper. Nor does one use the left hand to give or receive because this hand is reserved for body hygiene.

In the Tzeltal Indian culture of southern Mexico the female armpit and the shape of the upper leg must not be seen. When we conducted part of Mexico Summer Training Session in Wycliffe Jungle Camp there, we women wore blouses with sleeves and below-the-knee skirts, even on muddy survival trips. In North America, semi-nudity on beaches and in the media has become commonplace, but it is shocking to those Third World cultures whose people cover themselves completely even in the hottest climates.

The Tzeltal Indians shake hands by lightly brushing fingers with each other, and they are very reserved in facial expressions. A hearty new missionary arrived among them. One of the Tzeltal men described his first encounter with the newcomer. "He laughed at me and tried to throw me down," he reported.

Admitting ignorance is a problem in some cultures. In the rural areas of Mexico we have learned that when we ask directions, the local person will always point out a way, even if he has no idea where the place is. A Michigan professor going to lecture in Nigeria was advised never to answer class questions with "I don't know" because this would drop him sharply in the students' estimation.

Admitting blame also varies from culture to culture. In the Middle East it is unthinkable to deal directly to settle a difference. No one wants to lose face by acknowledging he is wrong. Using an intermediary is the only way to a solution, because it offers both parties a way out.

Remember that we look as confusing and illogical to a culture we enter as it looks to us. Marilyn Laszlo of Wycliffe tells a delightful story about using handkerchiefs as she worked with translation helpers along the Sepik River in Papua New Guinea. One day she overheard her helpers discussing in puzzled tones, "What is so valuable about the stuff the white woman blows out of her nose? She folds it carefully in a cloth and puts the cloth in her pocket to keep it."

Who Touches Whom?

We began to talk about cultural differences by asking, "How late is late?" Let's end with, "Who touches whom?"

In 1979 U.S. President Jimmy Carter arrived in Cairo to confer with Egyptian President Anwar Sadat. Carter expressed his Southern hospitality by kissing the president's wife when he was presented to her at the airport. The fierce negative Egyptian reaction to that kiss made more headlines than the international issues the two presidents planned to discuss. No one had told Carter that a Muslim wife is never touched by any man but her husband. Egypt felt insulted on behalf of its president's honor.

But men in Egypt often walk hand in hand or with their arms around each other. They kiss on both cheeks when they meet and when they part. That's not how it is in North America. It's important to know who may touch whom in different cultures.

Even if we stay in a new culture for years, we will never learn all of it, and we will always be something of an outsider. But we will be accepted and loved if our attitude is that of a servant.

Guidelines, Not Rules

There are no rule books or pat answers to prepare us for all the differences we will find when we enter a new setting. But there are guidelines, I believe. Let me suggest three:

1. We must love unconditionally and respect all kinds of people in their cultures and lifestyles, the way God did for us "while we were yet sinners."
2. We must be willing to live humbly within any culture "for the sake of the gospel," accepting and becoming part of it after the model of Christ when he came to us.

3. In matters where God's biblical teaching for all cultures differs from this new culture, we must model and teach—show and tell—what God intends, and then trust him for when and how he will bring persons to himself and work his changes in their behavior.

Paul sums it up when he says, "I have become all things to all men so that by all possible means I might save some. I do all this for the sake of the gospel, that I may share in its blessings" (1 Corinthians 9:22–23).

Relationships are the message of the gospel, the heart of evangelism, and the special challenge of cross-cultural ministry.

Just Go!

Let's end this chapter with some practical ways that you can experience cross-cultural ministry. Remember that it begins with an attitude of seeking out people different from you, here and now, with your "radar" out for them.

Without leaving your present setting, begin to spend time in one of these ways:

Find and befriend international students in public colleges and universities. Some go home and say that no one ever talked to them about Christ while they were studying in this free country.

Volunteer for a time each week at a refugee center, a tutoring program, a prison or juvenile detention center, a hospital, a soup kitchen, a food distribution program, a big brother or child welfare program, a drop-in center, a non-Christian nursing home or home for the elderly, a neighborhood center, a Bible club program for neighborhood children. Don't forget to look for cross-cultural opportunities where you live, shop, work, and study.

Widen your experience by planning the when and where of a short time away from home in a same-language cross-cultural setting. One Christmas vacation a student lived two weeks with homeless men in a downtown Chicago city mission. Go to the "hollers" of Appalachia or work a stint on disaster relief in a community devastated by tornado, earthquake, or flood. Be a counselor at a camp for minority children or special groups. Volunteer at a seamen's center in Montreal or Vancouver where ships of every nation dock. You don't need a special skill or assignment. Do anything that needs doing: sort clothes, fix things, transport people, cook food, play with children. Just major in showing love and being helpful as you learn how to be part of this new family and look for ways to show and tell what God has done for you.

George Verwer of Operation Mobilization had some strong advice when he spoke to students at Purdue University. "Get out of lopsided America," he said, "even if for a short time. People think you need a special call. All you need is an airline ticket. Get out, as a student, teacher, helper. Just get out!"

He was calling for young people to move one step farther, into another language group, another country. There are various summer programs for this. We are involved in several of them in Mexico and the Middle East. Youth with a Mission (YWAM) and Operation Mobilization (OM) are moving into new opportunities in Eastern Europe and begging for summer help. More and more churches are sending project groups to other parts of the world. Have you considered teaching English in China for a summer? Some of you might consider serving for a year or two in another culture as the Mormons do. Ask your own denomination first where you can be used, but you need not stop there. Inter-Cristo in Seattle, Washington, has 35,000 computerized ministry openings around the world. At present there are openings for teaching English in Egypt, Taiwan, Japan, the Bahamas, Mexico, and other countries. Apply to Wycliffe Bible Translators as a two-year Short Term Assistant (STA) with any skill you have—secretary, mechanic, hostess, nurse, computer operator, builder, handyman, child care aide. Talk to people who know of mission families desiring help, or ask a missionary whom your church supports.

Don't worry about money. God's people have the means to send others even if they do not go themselves. And God has surprising resources to compensate for the job paychecks you think you need to continue your college or university education.

Some of you will find the Lord assuring you about ministry in another culture where the needs are great and the rewards far outnumber the difficulties. Just go. And in your going, grow in Christ to be the person he will use as you build relationships and take your place with him in needy places of our global village. Involvement in missions will change your life forever.

Endnotes

Chapter 1

1. Quoted in *Uncle Cam: The Story of William Cameron Townsend,* by James and Marti Hefley (Waco, Texas: Word Books, 1974), p. 272.
2. Stanzas from a hymn by the author, "By Faith We Walk, and Not By Sight," 1975. All rights reserved.